The Enoch and E

Starting with

The Strange Affair of the Secret Groaty Pudding Recipe

Peter Yates

Sunday September 22nd 1963. Dear George –

It has been a strange week, last Monday I received through the post a letter from a firm of Tipton solicitors I had never heard of, Cooper, Baines and Crump. I was summoned to their office and would I call at three thirty on Friday afternoon the 20th inst. It is now Sunday evening the 22nd inst. and I have finally read and perhaps even digested some the contents of the sealed envelope I was given by Mr Crump –apparently the only surviving partner - when I entered his office.
With the formalities out of the way and my proffering of suitable proof of identity, Mr Crump, with some ceremony I have to say passed over to me an envelope which he said was to be given to me on the event of the death of the owner of said envelope, Job Morgan, a gentleman I had never heard of.
Job apparently was the illegitimate son of 'King' Ezekiah Morgan the legendary chip shop entrepreneur, he I had heard of but it came as a shock to discover he was a relative.
This came as a surprise to Mister Crump also as apparently the gentleman was an uncle or something of mine on my mother's side.
Job had lived and died in South Africa so although he was a half-brother or thereabouts to my mother and I subsequently discovered the black sheep of the family it came as no surprise that I had never heard of him
"Are you going to open the envelope?" enquired Mr Crump.
"When I get home," I answered.

Mr Crump found it hard to conceal his disappointment.

I have now read the contents of the envelope and quite frankly I find it hard to believe.

Having given it some thought I have decided to send it you for your opinion as it appears that the main characters in this astonishing saga are your nearest and dearest, your father Enoch and your uncle Eli – in fact it is narrated by your father, Enoch, not long before his passing over.

What do you think of it, is this the invention of some crazy old man – Ezekiah, not your father - steeped in chip fat or does 'it' really exist, and if so where is 'it'?

(Author's note - Perhaps we should explain what 'it' is, but first of all what constitutes groaty pudding? Many of you will know that it is made from groats of course, leeks, onions and beef stock – but – this particular recipe for groaty pudding contained two secret ingredients handed down through the Morgan family and unknown to anyone else. Yes, I know what these secret ingredients are and no I am not going to tell you, I have Morgan blood and I will not betray my heritage. I should correct a point in history, it is widely believed that the 'penny lick' glasses were invented so that day-trippers at the seaside could have a lick of ice cream from these glasses, all very true of course up to a point, but the origin of these penny lick glasses goes further back than Victorian seaside resorts. The original penny lick glass was a device invented so that the less well-to-do could savour the delights of groaty pudding at minimal expense.)

'It' is the secret groaty pudding recipe that purely through superstitious reasons was always referred to as 'it'.

'It' had always been kept in a safe at Brierley Hill town hall since time immoral, well, at least since 1899 when it was donated to the town by that very first Black Country chip shop owning Morgan – and less than illustrious grandfather to Ezekiah, Abraham Morgan.

One Monday morning shortly after adjusting her bra and zipping up her dress having been to Councillor Hardcastle's office for a cup of tea and a de-briefing if you will pardon the pun - young Lizzie Hill the town clerk, eager to get the notes of the last council meeting cleaned up – in other words removing the expletives – before they were read by the vicar, noticed that the safe door was open, in fact hanging from one hinge – she noticed this immediately, she was very observant and for this she subsequently received – in a private audience - a written citation from the Mayor Councillor Obediah Buckley and an invitation to a weekend for two on the rates in Aberystwyth; the records do not state whether she accepted but for years there used to be a paperweight with the legend 'present from Aberystwyth' printed across the base on the Mayor's desk. – and the secret groaty pudding recipe was missing.

Local gossips had it that it was either One Arm Louis and his hoodlums or Chugger Riley and his mob who had stolen the recipe, there was absolutely no proof whatsoever about either but rumour being rumour it wasn't long before it was an established fact. One Arm was favourite, he being more local to Brierley Hill than Chugger Riley..

Further investigation proved that the town hall had indeed been broken in to over the weekend, extensive and painstaking detective work by the local plod established this without question, evidence was eventually found including greasy chip papers, an empty Woodbine packet and the latest copy of Titbits. This could have emanated from the latest council meeting of course but as every councillor denied ever having read Titbits it was concluded that this rubbish had been selfishly left behind by the intruders – completely ignoring the waste paper baskets that there were there for that very purpose.

Conjecture was rife, who would want to steal part of Brierley Hill's priceless heritage, who would desecrate this sacred piece of Black Country lore? The word was it could only have been One Arm Louis Ferrari or Chugger Riley, that's who. As time went on the trail became cold, the police lost interest, the Chief Superintendent finally writing 'ay gorra clue' across the case notes in his best gothic script, adding the date, 15th October 1919. That, as they say was that…. Or was it?

The text of the document found in the envelope is as follows - dated June 1962. The contents of the envelope in full…..

Written in mine own hand over several days and relates to an event that started Thursday 10th September 1929. It is important that history should so record.
Enoch Stone.

(Author's note - We will continue in conventional script it being easier to read)
To whom it may concern –
I became involved with this affair quite by accident, my brother Eli of course could always get into trouble without even trying.
It started innocently enough, Eli was, as was his habit exiting the outdoor with a jug of ale. It was Saturday evening, being chapel he didn't like going into a public house on a Sunday so he brought home a jug every Saturday, the fact that by the time he started to drink it twenty four hours later it was as flat as a pancake didn't seem to bother him, mind you, as was well known, the beer at 'The Prince' is usually flat anyway, so who'd notice the difference.
It was almost certainly 'bitter', neither of us ever drank 'mild' in 'The Prince', not since we saw Bill the landlord pour the

slops into the mild barrel, apparently you can do this without anyone noticing but it can't be done with a bitter barrel it being a lighter colour and the dark mild slops of course would change its colour and the punters would smell a rat.

As Eli was attempting the challenging task of getting home without spilling any beer he was being gazed at intently from the other side of the road by a young lady, Jessie by name, who was standing underneath a gas lamp – she wasn't staring at him for professional reasons, she most certainly wasn't going to ask him if he wanted a good time, the working class were beneath her, well, some of the time, depending on their preference and by and large with a few exceptions, foremen, charge hands and the like, they certainly couldn't afford her; now had Eli noticed her he, all friendly like, would have smiled and shouted across to her, perhaps something like 'keep 'em crossed love, make 'em work for it!'.

Jessie studied Eli intently determined that she would be able to give a full description of him later… It had been a long time since any young lady had taken an interest in our Eli, if you don't include his wife but like most Black Country wives after the honeymoon period she rarely took an interest in her old man.

Jessie was frowning, she took off her gloves and stored them in a pocket of her imitation ocelot coat, she had a piece of paper and a pencil tucked down her bra, usually in case she needed to make a note of the name of a client she had become personally interested in and wanted to go private as it were, on her day off maybe, unknown to her boss.

She watched Eli as he made his way precariously along the street on his way home, precarious because his eyes were on the jug and not on the edge of the kerb off which he had nearly slipped a couple of times, although it has to be said he had never yet spilled his ale but there was always a first time.. Mind you he always took a gulp out of the jug before he left the pub so that such a disaster didn't happen, but typical Black

Country he always asked Bill to top the jug up again - a top-up for which he never paid.

Being careful not to be seen the young lady checked there were no paying punters heading her way then silently creeping along on the opposite side of the road dodging in and out of entries and gateways when necessary she followed Eli home; when she saw which front door he had entered she made a note of the address then with less secrecy made her way back to the lamp post she called her own, and woe betide any other young lady who had been daft enough to try to pinch her spot..

She read her notes and smiled.

She had news to impart later and knew that it should be worth her while…. Her boss would be very happy, he might even pay for her fish and chip supper.

 She spotted a well-dressed gent approaching, "fancy a good time, dearie?"

"I doe mind if I do," he replied. She tucked the piece of paper inside her bra… "Tha's private down there," she snapped to the gent who with his tongue hanging out was watching every move.

At last it was time to go, one late night wannabe punter was unlucky, "Yo'll 'ave to do it theesen, luv, I'm goin' 'ome."
And home she went – actually the private rooms above
 'The Continental' owned by Chugger Riley.

"It was 'im, I am telling thee it was 'im… Tony the Pizza, tall, scrawny, barmy looking, glasses fastened up with sticking plaster and wearing black boots, laces undone and a flat 'at. It was 'im I tell thee, it was definitely 'im, blimey Chugger, there cor be another daft bat like Tony the Pizza, con there, it 'as to be 'im."

Chugger Riley, now there's a name to conjour with.
Chugger owned the select restaurant and night club 'The
Continental' which sat artistically bathed in the floodlights
from the old coal yard on Tipton wharf, a romantic place if
you don't mind continually brushing off the coal dust from
your dish of the day. His nickname of 'Chugger' was a relic
from his days on the canal when he literally 'chugged' his
way round the British waterways system prior to having
ambitions – and access to a canal boat full of Brierley Crystal
which mysteriously went missing one Sunday somewhere
around Norton Canes. The boat re-appeared, but surprise,
surprise, it was empty. The cut glass was never seen again,
rumour had it it had been pre-ordered by a ready buyer from
America, the self-same buyer who would claim off his
insurance for the 'missing' cargo, thus scoring twice. Chugger
thought this over, why should he take all the risks so that a
foreigner could have all the bunce – less Chugger's
commission for a job well done - and this allegedly was the
start of Chugger Riley's climb through the ranks to the giddy
heights of night club owner and general up-market crook.
'The Continental' was the place to be seen, the place where
the trendies both young and old enough to know better of
Tipton and Great Bridge spent their time and their money, the
place where the great and the good could rub shoulders with
the top gangsters of the Black Country: they would park their
Edwardian versions of the later Morris Minors and their
Austin Allegros, then dressed in their Sunday best chapel suits
and top-of-the-range frocks from the nineteen and eleven rail
at Greys of Walsall saunter up the canal bank to 'The
Continental' to be met by Alfie, the half-deaf concierge where
they would tip a ten bob note, or a quid if anyone was looking
and Alfie would escort them to a table; it wasn't cheap, a
bowl of mushy peas was the equivalent to a day's wages in
the next door foundry, but still people went if only so the next
door neighbour can whisper "'im next door an' 'is fancy piece

was there again last night…. It'll all end in tears, you mark my words… 'Is missus is bound to find out sooner or later."
Unknown to most of 'The Continental's' clientele was what lay beyond the little door in the back wall marked 'no admittance'.
Councillors, bookmakers, bishops, their friends and friends of their friends, if they could prove they were loaded enough were allowed through this door into the strip club which lay beyond. This was the main source of Chugger's income and like that more famous monument to that particular form of artistic endeavour 'The Windmill' in London it never closed.
Jessie took off her ocelot coat and stretched out on the divan that sat along Chugger's office wall directly below a painting of 'Paradise' a long since defunct canal boat that once upon a time in a different life had been the pride and joy of his Uncle Cornelius.
Chugger was having difficulty concentrating on her words, her legs kept getting in the way.
"Am yo listenin' Chug?"
He shook himself free of his erotic thoughts….
"Ey..what was yo' sayin'?"
"I said it must be 'im."
Chugger nodded his head, from the description he was inclined to agree, how many dumbass's of that description can there be in Tipton?
"He must be just out the nick, Jess, I heard he was inside, One Arm Louis must have sprung him… or else Tony the Pizza's been a good boy and earned his parole, either way he'll still be Louis's number one, Tony is the only gang member One Arm Louis trusts, if only 'cos in my opinion 'e ay got the brains to try to take over the operation, therefore he will be the only gang member who will know the location of the secret groaty pudding recipe, One Arm wouldn't dare tell anybody else. I'll get the boys to find our friend Tony the

Pizza and bring 'im in… With my powers of persuasion he will soon tell us where the recipe is."

Jessie smiled, Chugger will be thrilled to bits with what she had down her bra, and you know what I mean… "I think I might be able to help you there, Chug."

Jessie poked around inside her bra for the piece of paper which did nothing for Chugger's state of mind. In fact it took his mind right off wanting to thank her for using her brains for a change.

"This is 'is address, you say, Woolley's Yard, number seven?"

"That's it," she was disappointed Chugger couldn't be bothered to thank her, although in all truth it was her own fault, well, her boobs anyway.

"It's just round the corner from…."

He cut her off. "I know where it is, Tony the Pizza has certainly gone down in the world living in a two up two down and one at the back, not the most salubrious abode for one of One Arm Louis senior torpedoes, but I suppose he has to get back on his feet if he's just come out the nick, something you should think about, Jess, getting back on your feet you're not getting any younger."

Jessie ignored the jibe, after all there were years left in Jessie's attractions yet – in her opinion.

The boys as Chugger calls them were duly despatched to knock on the door of number seven Woolley's yard the following tea time and invite Tony the Pizza to call on his old friend Chugger – meaning right now - and there wasn't an option.

There was no answer, Tony/Eli was out. The boys were not best pleased, this was eating into their drinking time, but the boss said they had to bring in One Arm's second in command so that was what they had to do, if not the boss could get pretty nasty.

They sat in the car prepared to wait as long as necessary.

Deggo, the driver was nodding off when his mate Jimmy saw 'Tony' saunter down the yard and disappear up the entry.

"At last", he muttered; he shook Deggo awake.

"Stir your stumps, he's here, gone up the entry, let's get him." Making sure they were armed, a shooter in the ribs would shift the balance if this loser started arguing, they went up the entry and banged on the back door of number seven.

It was several seconds before they heard a movement, the bolt was undone and the door creaked open. Standing there chewing on a sun dried tomato and mozarella pizza was the spitting image of the description Jessie had given to Chugger, there was no mistake. Gormless looking, broken spectacles, zits – which Jessie had failed to spot, if you'll pardon the pun, in the dark – and flat cap. It was Tony the Pizza all right.

"Get your coat, Chugger wants to see you," announced Deggo without bothering with the formality of introducing himself.

"And he wants to see you right now," added Jimmy.

"Cor come now, I'm bottlin' me 'ome brew," spluttered Eli/Tony spitting bits of pizza all down Jimmy's waistcoat.

Deggo smiled, "sorry about your home brew pal but Chugger says he wants to see you now not when you feel like it."

Quick as a flash they grabbed one arm each, twisted them up behind the back of their unfortunate victim and frogmarched him down the entry and threw him in the back of the car.

Job done, and back to base with a present for the boss.

Blindfolded, Eli/Tony was bundled through the back door of 'The Continental' and up the stairs to Chugger's private apartment.

"This ay very funny, my 'ome brew will 'ave gone off if I doe put the corks up the neck of the bottles."

"Shut up, or I'll put a cork up you and it won't be up your neck," snapped Jimmy, still a tad miffed about the tomato sauce – Eli had always said that sun dried tomatoes lacked something so he always drenched his pizzas in tomato sauce - all down his waistcoat to say nothing of the as yet to be noticed nub end of chipolata sausage wedged in the top pocket; known for his snazzy waistcoats was Jimmy.

Deggo rang the bell and entered without waiting for Chugger to open the door. It was best they got Tony the Pizza out of sight as soon as possible.

The captive was pushed down into the depths of a luxurious armchair and the blindfold was removed.

He blinked, it took a while for his eyes to focus.

He was in a room the like of which he had never seen, plush curtains, velvet covers on the sofa, even tassels on the lamps which sat on the highly polished mahogany table. There was even carpet on the floor, a sure sign of excessive sophistication.

Chugger stood immediately in front of Eli, he smiled, it was not a nice smile, and introduced himself in his very best speaking voice, the one he usually reserved for the Masons.

"Chugger Riley, boss of all the bosses here in Tipton and thereabouts, and you are number one loser Tony the Pizza, loser because you are on the wrong side...."

Eli tried to interrupt but the pressure on the back of his neck exerted by Jimmy's shooter seemed to indicate that right now wasn't the time. Chugger continued, "Your boss, One arm Louis has something I want, the secret groaty pudding recipe, he stole it... Took it from the safe in Brierley Hill town hall, an audacious robbery but a dangerous one, dangerous for both him and the idiots who were with him on the night of the caper... One of them wouldn't have been you, Tone, would it?"

Eli wasn't given the chance to answer, Chugger was in full flow. "I intend to give a dinner for the civic dignitaries and all my mates in three weeks' time; in fact it has always been my ambition to hold a prestigious golf tournament on my own private golf course followed by a slap-up dinner, so in three weeks' time for all my good friends hereabouts, and thereabouts, with the inevitable one or two layabouts that's what I'm doing here at 'The Continental', and the main course will be groaty pudding made to the secret recipe... Even though I don't – for the moment – have the recipe in my hand I don't see that as a problem, do you?

Once again Eli wasn't allowed to speak.

"The Mayor had agreed to be guest of honour, in return he had promised to release the secret recipe just for this one grand dinner...."

Chugger noticed the tomato sauce marks on Jimmy's waistcoat and 'tut-tutted', using a forefinger and thumb he extracted the chipolata from Jimmy's pocket and flicked it across the room where it landed perfectly in the waste paper basket; if only my putting was that good, he sighed.... "If you are coming to my 'do' Jimmy boy you had best bring your own napkin, I don't want my monogrammed silk jobbies stained in tomato sauce, it won't come out." He turned his attention back to Eli and continued.

"But your guvnor has nicked it, and I don't like that. Your job young Tony is to take a message back to One arm Louis, if I don't get that secret recipe inside forty eight hours, he will see his little band of helpers get even littler, one by one... Until he will be the only him left, and even One Arm Louis won't muster a lot of clout without a gang, wouldn't you say?"

Once again Eli was cut off but this time by the door opening and the entrance of Jessie and her ocelot coat. She was just about to go out on the street but needed some pound notes, every now and again a punter who'd maybe had a good day on the horses paid with a fiver and wanted change.

Chugger was in a good mood, "Well done Jessie, thanks to you we are in the company of Tony the Pizza, One Arm Louis' main man."

Jessie stepped a little nearer, she needed her glasses but was too vain to wear them. She peered at Eli and groaned.

"This ay Tony the Pizza Chugger, I ay gorra clue who 'e is but it ay Tony."

Chugger's good mood – and posh accent - disappeared, "Yo said it was, yo dozy mare, yo even gid me 'is address!"

"It was dark an' I was on t'other side of the street, any road up this ay Tony the Pizza, I should know, I've shared a pizza with Tony many a time behind the co-op when he's been strapped for cash and couldn't pay."

Deggo and Jimmy wondered if they had made a mistake, but no, their instructions had been explicit, call at number seven Woolley's yard and bring back the bloke who lives there. Chugger couldn't blame them.

"So, who the 'ell is 'e?" muttered Deggo.

"Eli Stone, late of His Majesty's foot and mouth and famous for me 'ome brew… which incidentally will be flat by now 'cos it ay been corked.. Wouldst mind telling me what is going on?"

Chugger was open-mouthed, fuming he turned on Jessie. "Yo to'd me… Yo guaranteed this was Tony the Pizza…. I'll sort yo out later, don't make any plans for next week yo wo feel well enough, meanwhile what the 'ell are we gonna to do about 'im?"

Jimmy coughed, he ventured to speak.

"We'll have to get rid of him boss, you told him all about the secret groaty pudding recipe, all about 'The Continental' connection, and if he tells his mates and the plod find out and come a-calling on the night of the big nosh-up you'll be in dead lumber – especially from the other mobsters who might object to being arrested for complicity in the breaking and entering of Brierley Hill town hall and the theft of the groaty pudding recipe, even though it wasn't them what done it."

Yes, I did tell this idiot, thought Chugger, I told him everything, rather careless of me.

"Lock 'im in the outside toilet while we think of what to do with 'im, maybe we can ship 'im out after midnight… Bump 'im off and hide 'is body under a tarp on a canal boat, 'e might not be noticed until Stourbridge."

13

It seemed like a good plan so poor old Eli – actually he was only twenty seven – was once again blindfolded, he was also gagged and tied up. Jimmy and Deggo carried him to the old outside toilet which had become redundant ever since Chugger had seen fit to install one of those new-fangled indoor fancy gadgets and they were none too gentle as they threw him in.

Jessie spotted her chance and left, a bit smartish, she had Chugger's wrath to look forward to later and that wasn't a pleasant thought, famous for his wrath was Chugger; maybe a few half-handsome punters might take her mind off the ordeal yet to come – 'half-handsome'…round here?

Standing under her gas lamp she was a very unhappy girl, partly for herself but also for that poor innocent mug she had virtually condemned to death and a less than scenic ride in a canal boat to Stourbridge…

It was just after the second punter had paid, he didn't even tip, when Jessie decided what to do. It was her fault this Eli chap was in trouble so she had to be the one to get him out of it. She felt a little better… Josie, a relative newcomer to the scene approached. Now normally Jessie would have shooed her off, this was her gas lamp and no-one else was allowed near, but on this occasion Jessie thought that Josie might come in useful. She told Josie that if she promised to leave this patch and go back to where ever she was normally she could stay on Jessie's turf for this one night only, on the understanding that she – Josie – would clear off when Jessie returned the following night, and not take any of Jessie's regulars with her.

Jessie's pitch was regarded as one of the best in the town so Josie agreed immediately, thinking that Jessie was doing her a favour, when actually it was she who was doing the favour, her 'occupancy' of the gas lamp ensured that other girls were kept away, girls who might not have vacated the pitch on the following day as easy as Josie, in fact there were one or two who might have made a fight out of it.

Leaving her pitch in good hands Jessie set off on her mission.

The Great Escape

It was easy for Jessie to make her way round the back of the club, even in the dark, she had served her apprenticeship amongst the dustbins and rubbish bags and she knew every doorway. The outside lavvy looked deserted but this poor bloke was supposed to be in there; she tried to peer through the moon shaped ventilation hole in the door but she could see nothing. Trying the door, expecting to find it locked she managed to open it slightly without a sound. She then realised that it wasn't locked because there was no lock; even under the stress of the occasion she chuckled, did that mean that in the old days before the advent of the posh new inside loo if you were in here you had to either sing or whistle if you thought you heard someone approaching?

She stopped chuckling when she saw Eli sitting on the loo, a pathetic figure done up like a kipper, blindfolded and gagged, he couldn't have looked worse.

Jessie carefully removed the blindfold first, then the gag.

"Am yo okay, cock, have they 'urt thee?"

Eli shook his head, it was easier than trying to speak.

Jessie undid the rope holding his arms then with some help from Jessie Eli untied the ropes that were causing his legs to go to sleep the ropes were that tight.

He massaged his legs and arms. "I suppose a thank you is in order, miss, although I have no idea who you are… Wait a minute, haven't I seen that coat somewhere?"

The penny dropped. "I 'ave, I've seen that coat afore, is it yo what stands by the gas lamp opposite 'The Prince?"

Jessie nodded, "I'm Jessie but the introductions can wait, we have to get out of here…."

Leading the way Jessie crept out of the lavvy and re-traced her steps back to the alley behind the club.

"Mind the dustbins, if you knock them over we're in trouble."

But he didn't, he was careful, even the luscious sight of Jessie's rear chassis ticking over from side to side wasn't enough to make him knock over a dustbin.

Fancy, he thought, I have been rescued by a lady of the night.

It was several streets before Jessie slowed down, then she ducked into an alley, yet another location where juniors learn their craft. She pulled Eli in beside her, he didn't mind that she smelled lovely.

"We should be safe now, they won't come this way even if they discover you are missing."

Eli's brain had somehow started working again, "who are they, and if I am safe, who am I safe from?"

"You saw him, Chugger Riley, that's who."

"Yes, but why... what have I done?"

"Absolutely nothing my love, you have done absolutely nothing at all."

He frowned, "Then why....?"

"Mistaken identity, that's why."

Jessie refrained from telling him that she was the one who initially mistook him for Tony the Pizza, now didn't seem the right time.

She explained that Chugger wasn't happy and an unhappy gangster can be a bit scary.

Eli's brain was starting to work. "So... as well as being Eli Stone of the drains department of the local council I'm also a look-a-like gangster in a rival gang to Chugger Riley by the name Tony the Pizza.... catchy name, Tony the Pizza, not a drains department name I have to say but definitely a good gangster name"

"It'll be catchy all right if Chugger catches up with thee."

 Under different circumstances it might have been quite exciting, but Eli was wide awake enough to realise that he was in some trouble and the only person who appeared to be on his side was this girl who he daren't tell his missus about.

"Do you think it's safe enough to go home?"

"Don't be a mug, that's the first place they'll look, damn it man they know the address, that's where they picked you up."

"There is no-where else I can go, I'm on the run then, ay I?."

"Make that, we are on the run, I don't fancy what Chugger might have planned for me later, but that is another story. Do you have a car?"

"Doe be daft, lass, I've on'y gorra tandem."

It gets worse she thought, here I am on the run from Chugger Riley and it looks like I'm on a tandem!

"Doe look so glum lass, me and our kid went to Blackpool on the tandem, it ay that bad."

Jessie frowned, "I ay goin' to Blackpool on a tandem we'll 'ave to find somewhere a bit nearer…"

She had a thought…

"Yo mentioned yo'r missus, will 'er report thee missin' if yo doe go 'ome?"

"Er wo know, 'er's at 'er mothers, we 'ad a row."

"What about, not that it's anything to do with me?"

"We 'ad a row about the number of times 'er buggers off to 'er mothers… especially just after we've 'ad a row."

"When's 'er cumin back?"

"Wo be for ages, 'er con be gone for a fortnit."

Jessie had a little think, "It seems to me the best thing we con do is get yo'r tandem, pop round to yo'r kid's 'ouse, tell 'im what's 'appened and clear off to Scotland."

Eli looked at his companion. "Bit drastic, ay it, Scotland, that's further than Blackpool!"

"Is it?"

"Shouldn't we try to find this bloke wot I've been mistook for and turn 'im over to this Chugger wotsit?"

Jessie nodded, it was obvious really, to get them both off the hook they had to find Tony the Pizza and turn him over to

Chugger, actually any member of the rival gang would do but Jessie didn't know their names or where they lived so Tony it would have to be. She glanced across at her new friend and sighed, wouldn't he be a bit weedy in a scrap, if it came to a scrap? Of course it would come to a scrap, Tony the Pizza isn't likely to be lured into the warm tender clutches of Chugger Riley purely be charm alone.

"Where dun yo keep the tandem?"

"At our kid's, 'e's got a shed to keep it in an' I ay."

Jessie sighed, at least they were doing something, if only collecting a tandem….. A tandem?

Actually it wasn't far, only about three streets away, yet another two up and two down and one at the back.

Enoch opened the scullery door and waved his visitors into the front parlour, he was frowning, who was this flashy woman with his brother, Eli had never bothered with women, especially women who wore stilts for shoes and skirts up to their earrings, she was wearing enough makeup to paint the wash house; it had always been said that Eli would never have married if his future bride to be hadn't proposed without the option to refuse.

Jessie took in the room, homely but bare, no flash, she was used to flash living with Chugger – well, not maybe living with him but she did provide some home comforts every now and again. Sitting here casting her eye over the Staffordshire flat-back figures on the mantle-piece, the inevitable Aspidistra in its ceramic pot in the window and the highly polished brass and copper companion stand guarding the fireplace made her feel quite depressed, and actually rather home sick. She had been brought up in a house similar to this in a similar street in a similar town not all that far away. Her mother had given up the ghost at forty and drowned herself in the canal having spent fifteen years struggling to make ends meet; Jessie's father – to whom no blame could have been attached for his wife's demise, in the coroner's opinion - even though he had never shown any affection for his family – met up with a widow from Ackermen Street and moved out, never giving a backward glance, which upset his kids somewhat. The son Ernie joined the army and was never seen again, the youngest daughter ran away with a Salvation Army activist and Jessie, having told the landlord that she didn't want the house anymore re-located to a one room bed-sit and a gas lamp, it seemed the logical thing to do, at least it was a living. She was nineteen at the time. On the whole she had no regrets, although sitting here now in this elm seated armchair by the fire which would have been more comforting had it been lit the memories came flooding bask and she was shocked to realise that she missed them. She was still miles away when Eli introduced her to his brother Enoch, who being not so innocent in the ways of the world had worked out in a second that Jessie was no better than she ought to be although her status, be that amateur or professional was still unclear.

Eli nudged her back to the present and introduced her; it was she who started telling Enoch of the mess they were in. Enoch sat open-mouthed, astonished, partly because of the amazing story he was listening to and partly because of her legs off which he couldn't take his eyes, what had his dopey brother got himself into? Whatever it was, with legs like that it wasn't all bad.

"It wor my fault, our kid, I cor 'elp it if this Tony the Pizza looks like me."

"The thing is" continued Jessie – she had seen Enoch's eyes glued to her legs and slewed round in the chair so that he could get the best effect - "Chugger Riley thinks that our Eli is Tony the Pizza and unless we can deliver the real Tony your brother will live in fear for the rest of his life – which may not be a long one."

Enoch shook his head dismissively, "Eli's used to livin' in fear, he married Thelma."

"Any road," butted in Eli, "We need the tandem, we 'ave to get as far away as we con, otherwise I wo be back 'ome when Thelma comes back from 'er mother's, if yo get my drift."
"Listen, our kid, if yo clear off – where'm yo thinking of goin' by the way?"
"Scotland" said one,
"Blackpool." Said the other.
Enoch sighed, "the fust thing yo've got to do is meck yo'r mind up which way yo'm goin' otherwise one on thee will be pedalling to Scotland and t'other will be peddlin' to Blackpool, the tandem will get confused and neither of thee will get past the end of the street."
Eli nodded, his brother was always the one with the brains.
Enoch continued, "besides, if yo do go to Blackpool – it ay too crowded at this time of year and it's nearer than Scotland - how will thee find this Tony the Pizza, it ay very likely yo'm gonna find 'im up Blackpool Tower."
They hadn't considered that. It was make your mind up time, do they go into hiding in Blackpool and never come home, Jessie thought that might work, there might be more punters in Blackpool and they might have more disposable income, although finding an available gas lamp might be a problem, especially in a classy joint like Blackpool.
It also appealed to Eli, but for different reasons, it might mean he would never see Thelma and her mother ever again, he nodded, yes Blackpool certainly had its attractions.
"The downside of running away," continued Enoch, "might mean that this Chugger Riley might try to take out his anger on Thelma and her mother, it wouldn't be a pretty sight."
Eli shuddered, "I already I feel sorry for 'im, up against Thelma and her mother 'e's got no chance."
Jessie had been thinking, hard.
"We'll stay," announced Jessie, making a momentous decision, she was still feeling guilty about fingering Eli.

"We 'ave to clear your brother's name, besides, until we have sorted this I cor go back to work, Chugger will 'ave every gas lamp in the town watched."

Enoch frowned, "why…..? The penny dropped, "Oh, I see."

Eli was slumped in a chair by the fire, "What are we goin' to do, our kid?"

Jessie opened the scullery door, "the first thing is have a cup of tea… I'll be mother."

Enoch managed to close the door to the scullery after Jessie had left the parlour.

"Who the hell is she," he hissed, "and what about this gas lamp malarkey, yo'r missus'll kill thee."

Eli had been thinking, "I doe care what my missus will do, I ay bothered, I 'ope 'er stops at 'er mothers 'til Christmas."

Enoch didn't like this. "Somebody is goin' to tell 'er yo'm gaddin' about with a trollop an' 'er'll be back with an oversize rolling pin."

"I doe care, an' Jessie ay a trollop, she might earn her livin' a bit different to the rest of the stuck-up cows round here but 'er ay a trollop…. Any road, even if our Thelma finds out I'll be long gone by the time 'er cums wum, wo I?"

Jessie came back into the room, "I cor find no sugar."

"That's cos we ay got none, my missus says that like trifle and tinned pears it's an unnecessary extravagance except for Christmas, besides we cor afford it this week I ay done no overtime."

They sat and drank their tea.

"I've been thinkin'," muttered Enoch. "Yo'm trying to find this Tony the Pizza… What about if yo let 'im find thee? Put the word out down the canal, somebody will blab and this geezer wo be able to resist trying to find out what all the fuss is about. And if you do that neither of you need go to Blackpool… nor Scotland, although yo' might find the tandem 'andy for gettin' round the sheds along the canal."

"So we still need the tandem?"

Enoch nodded, Jessie was disappointed.

"In the meantime," Jessie uncrossed her legs, "I need a place to stay and so does Eli, he can't go home, Chugger will have a man on the doorstep waiting for him, and when I don't go back to The Continental later Chugger will soon realise that I have scarpered.

Enoch shook his head, he noticed his hands were shaking, "I'm sorry, gel, but yo cor stay 'ere, my missus'll be back from her sister's soon and if 'er finds somebody like yo – no offence – in our parlour all three of we will need a place to stay.

Eli smiled, he was having one of his rare flashes of inspiration. "What about yo'r allotment?"

Enoch was yet to catch up, "What about my allotment?"

Eli was on a roll, "it 'as an 'ut!"

"What?" Jessie was as far behind as Enoch.

Eli sighed, "every allotment has a place to store tools and stuff…. An 'ut! We con stay in the 'ut.

Enoch caught up. "Oh, an' 'ut! The 'ut on my allotment… got it, grand idea, our kid, there's even that old sofa in there that used to be Grannie Evans's before the Good Lord took 'er', it's still a good'un, more or less, cousin Elsie wanted it for 'er eldest what was getting wed but we said that Grannie Evans had left it to we and 'er couldn't 'ave it."

Jessie was open-mouthed, were these two barmpots asking her to live in a hut on an allotment – with or without a sofa?"

"There's an old army cooker an' all, we wo starve," laughed Eli, "in fact it might be quite cosy."

The vision in Jessie's mind's eye didn't include cosy in the description. A tandem, an old sofa – which allegedly was still a good'un more or less - and an old army cooker, what luxury, what bliss!

The only problem with this, as far as Enoch was concerned was it would be his brother Eli who was going to spend the night – in fact probably several nights - cooped up in his hut on the allotment with this girl with all these legs and not himself. Some people have all the luck.

It took a little while to extract the tandem from the shed in the back garden which in turn brought to light a couple of army blankets, a bit musty but better than nothing, and an oil lamp. "It'll be like 'ome from'ome," giggled Eli, "just thee and me and no Thelma…. Better than 'ome from 'ome in fact."

It occurred to Jessie that against all the odds would Eli try his luck with her once they had settled down for the night… and if he did, did she make him pay?

She shrugged, Eli was now a kind of friend, and friends get mate's rates so maybe she could do a buy one and get one free arrangement? Anyway, she thought, it was me what got him into this pickle so maybe I owe him one.

Now came the hard part, getting on the tandem complete with oil lamp and army blankets, but somehow they did, giving Enoch one last tantalising leer at Jessie's legs. Actually there wasn't a cross bar on the back it was built for a man and a woman so there was no operational necessity for Jessie to hitch her skirt up quite as far as she did but why not, she figured, they were borrowing this man's allotment hut and his tandem in order to stay clear of that maniac Chugger Riley - and therefore maybe live a little longer - so giving Enoch a quick thrill was a small price to pay.

Home from Home – more or less

Actually the hut wasn't too bad once Eli had banged on the floor a few times to get rid of the mice and the creepy-crawlies.

The infamous sofa was resplendent in its past glory, an old kitchen table filled the centre of the floor and there were various odds and ends of crockery and cutlery littering its surface, some of it clean. A cupboard door unveiled a bottle of

Camp coffee, a packet of tea and a tin of condensed milk and very little else, it would be a food free night.

According to Eli there was a cold water standpipe outside only a few yards away and a portable toilet by the allotment entrance gate. It didn't get any better, but as Jessie kept telling herself at least for now they were safe.

Jessie refused coffee with or without that disgusting milk and settled down on the sofa expecting Eli to want to want to join her but after he had drunk his coffee he pushed a load of mucky magazines off an old deck chair in the corner that had come from a drunken escapade by coach to Rhyl a few years ago – it still had RUC on the back - then pulling one of the army blankets up under his chin he tucked his legs underneath him, pulled his cap down over his eyes and closed them.

"Goodnight, miss."

Miss….miss? "Goodnight Eli."

Much to Jessie's amazement - and she was surprised to realise her disappointment – Eli didn't stir all night.

Jessie couldn't sleep, her mind was frantically trying to work out just how they were going to get out of this mess, Chugger would be scouring the town for them, Eli in his innocence didn't seem to realise the gravity of the situation: as far as Chugger was concerned Eli was Tony the Pizza, a senior member of One Arm Louis' gang and therefore the key to getting back the secret groaty pudding recipe in time for the grand banquet and nothing was going to stop him, it was a matter of pride to Chugger, he daren't fail or he would lose his status with the other gangs, and status was everything. Eventually, getting a glimpse of an idea her brain slowed down enough to enable her to get at least an hour or two's sleep.

Overnight the half idea Jessie's tired brain had come up with had festered away and when she finally stirred she felt very much better.

It was a silent breakfast, Eli had slipped out just after dawn and brought back two large bacon sandwiches wrapped in newspaper from the transport café, then after making tea he gently nudged Jessie awake. In the night she had shrugged off her top, bra and skirt, Eli shuddered and covered her with the army blanket. Actually Jessie was wide awake and realised what he had done, she smiled, did that make him a gentleman…. Or simply a geezer terrified of his missus? She decided to eat her bacon sandwich before dressing herself much to Eli's discomfort.

"You forgot the tomato sauce, Eli."

"Sorry."

The sun was up, it was time to decide what to do, they couldn't simply stay in the hut all day, besides some of the other allotment holders would be turning up soon and if they saw a woman come out of the hut at this time of the morning tongues would soon start to wag and before they had put the kettle on Eli's missus would be in full possession of the facts, at least the facts as the allotment holders saw them -

'Oooh, I say, Thelma love, as much as I 'ate to be the bearer of bad news - an' yo know I ay a gossip - but I've just 'eard yo'r Eli couldn't wait for thee to go to your mothers, afore he spent the night with a tart in Enoch's hut down the allotment; I allus said yo should 'ave gid that sofa to Cousin Elsie!'

Guilty as charged, what more did his missus need to know? Fortunately Jessie was almost fully dressed when Enoch turned up, he had told his lady wife he had some jobs to do on the allotment and she, always grateful when he cleared off out of her way had readily agreed.

Jessie was pulling up her skirt just too late to give Enoch a glimpse of her knickers as Enoch came through the door, he grinned, made a rude gesture in the direction of Eli who didn't get it, sighed and un-wrapped his contribution to breakfast, three more bacon sandwiches, complete with tomato sauce this time.

Jessie called the meeting to order, you have to find Tony the Pizza she said, then you have to deliver him to Chugger. "Ang on," interrupted Enoch, "*'you'*, I notice you said *'you'*, not *'we'*, never *'we'*."

Jessie didn't see the problem, "yes, *'you'*... You, you and Eli will have to find Tony the Pizza and get him to Chugger Riley, I cor do it, Tony will only think I'm chasin' after 'im for a spot of hanky panky and as Tony never pays he can stuff it, I lost enough money last night – I may even have lost my gas lamp an' all, some chancer might be claiming squatter's rights unless Josie sends 'em off an' I cor see that, 'er bein' new at the game - I will have to go to work tonight and stake my claim on that lamp, you two will be on your own, so yes, you will have to find Tony the Pizza, I have a living to earn.... it has to be you two."

"But we don't know what he looks like," groaned Eli.

"Of course you do," she sighed, "he looks like thee!"

That was it, they agreed, reluctantly it has to be said, Enoch and Eli would put the word about that they wanted to see Tony the Pizza at the allotment at midnight, Jessie's idea, meanwhile Jessie would re-stake her claim to the gas lamp, they would meet up at the hut at eleven thirty and wait for Tony, assuming he turns up. If he didn't it could only mean he didn't get the message and they would have to repeat the procedure the following day.

"What my missus is going to say about me bein' 'ere at the allotment in the middle of the night I dread to think," Enoch had the feeling of doom that only a black country working class man can have, or at least that's what they think, that they are the only married men in captivity condemned to spend a whole lifetime in purgatory, except on Sundays when it is chapel, although according to some it is very similar, certainly there's no ale.

Eli shook his head, "No, 'er wo, ay it a sayin' round these parts that sweet pea seeds – especially them what am destined for the annual show when cash can be won, yo know, cash what can be spent on chocolates, make-up an' stuff, for the best wife in the world ....am best sown by moonlight?" He tilted his head slightly and smiled demurely, Jessie giggled. Enoch frowned, "I day know that!"

Jessie giggled again. "I think Eli just made it up. Well done, Eli, yo ay as daft as thee look." Jessie was beginning to re-evaluate her opinion of Eli.

Eli grinned, "I might be cabbage looking but I ay green".

No, thought Jessie, no, I don't think you are.

Their master plan was complete, Enoch and Eli would scour the pubs, caffs and billiard halls making it known that Tony the Pizza would learn something to his advantage if he went to the allotment that night at midnight, third hut on the left as you go in.

Surely someone would make sure he knew, if only so that if Tony the Pizza was coming into money they might remind him who told him he was wanted.

The only problem was – it wasn't Tony the Pizza who got the message, Tony was at the races at Cheltenham, it was his boss One Arm Louis – and he wasn't going to wait until midnight before knocking on the door of the third hut on the left in the allotments…..

It had been just before lunch time when One Arm Louis had a visitor…

"I'm telling thee, One Arm, there's this geezer goin' round asking for Tony the Pizza, 'e was in the caff not long since an' whoever 'e is says that if Tony turns up at this particular 'ut on the allotment at midnight 'e might learn summat to 'is advantage."

One Arm Louis was puzzled, 'might learn summat to 'is advantage', that's classic lawyer speak is that, does this mean Tony had an elderly aunt who has snuffed it and left him with a load of money, and if so would it be enough for Tony to launch a takeover bid for the gang? One Arm had always suspected Tony of being a tad ambitious in that direction, a bit thick, granted but is he cute enough to bribe the others in the gang to vote against One Arm at the next monthly meeting? One Arm Louis had another queer thought…Since when did solicitors read the will in an allotment hut at midnight?

When the recipient has a lot to hide, that's when… I'll kill 'im, thought One Arm Louis, but not until I find out exactly how much mazuma he has come in to and how I get my hands on it…. No, maybe bumping 'im off is a bit drastic, I know I'll offer 'im a partnership…Then when I've got me 'onds on the loot then I'll bump 'im off.

A visit to this allotment hut would be in order, no, extremely necessary…. before Tony got the message, and long before midnight.

The moon was hiding behind a dark and menacing cloud, maybe it was going to rain later, as One Arm Louis along with one of his gang, Bloxwich 'Arry crept into the allotments; they counted off the huts, one - two - three- then making sure they had an un-interrupted view of the third hut on the left made themselves comfortable behind a water butt outside the first of the huts.

"What's the time, 'Arry?"

Bloxwich 'Arry checked his watch, it was eleven fifteen, too early maybe but better than too late. One Arm Louis extracted a hip flask and took a slug it might keep out the cold.

Bloxwich 'Arry was disappointed.

"Quiet….!"

They listened…. Eventually, yes they could hear voices..

Coming through the allotment gate were three dark figures, not easy to distinguish but who else would it be at this time of night, it must be Tony the Pizza and two of his cronies….

"I'll kill 'im," whispered One Arm.

The three figures passed very close to the two men hiding, One Arm was shocked to realise that he recognised a pair of legs, a pair of legs he had long wanted to get acquainted with but due to pressure of business – and his wife's excessive vigilance – he had never managed to, there was no mistake, the legs belonged to Jessie… one of Chugger Riley's tarts. One Arm frowned, what is going on?

The moon managed to poke out from the cloud just long enough for Bloxwich 'Arry to clock the faces… Yes, it was Jessie, a young lady whose legs 'Arry had never made the acquaintance of either, but this was solely because he never had any money, the second person he had no idea about but the third was easy, it was Tony the Pizza.

"That's 'im, boss, Tony the Pizza… I wonder why he never told you he was comin' 'ere?"

One Arm knew why, Tony wanted to keep the news of his aunt's fortune to himself that's why.

"What shall we do, boss?"

"Wait until they have gone in the hut…. That one you didn't recognise must be the lawyer what's come to read the Will."

"What Will, boss?"

"Don't worry your little 'ead about it 'Arry, it's high finance you wouldn't understand.

Bloxwich 'Arry didn't understand low finance so there was no point in trying to explain the situation.

"Sit tight until they have had chance to settle down, then we burst in and surprise 'em."

Bloxwich 'Arry frowned, "Shouldn't we 'ave back-up, boss?"

"You are the back-up, idiot."

"Oh yeh… Sorry boss."

Inside the hut they were ready, it only needed for Tony the Pizza to arrive and all would be sorted… Assuming he had received the message of course.

"Of course he'll 'ave got the message," muttered Eli, "Me and Enoch went in every pub and caff for miles, if Tony the Pizza never got the message it means he day 'ave a sarnie nor a cuppa all day long."

They had salvaged a good supply of rope, a large red spotted handkerchief for a gag and had 'borrowed' the old bentwood chair from the next door allotment to tie Tony the Pizza to. All they would have to do then was go and fetch Chugger Riley, job done.

It all depended on Tony the Pizza.

Eli heard a noise outside… "Shush, I think I hear summat." Enoch heard it as well.

Then Jessie heard someone approaching on the door.

Knock… knock….

"It's 'im, 'e's 'ere."

"As long as it ay my missus, we'm safe enough," muttered Enoch.

"Tony the Pizza can be really dangerous," whispered Jessie.

"'E ay met my missus."

Jessie opened the door, she caught her breath as she saw One Arm Louis and Bloxwich 'Arry standing there, One Arm was smiling, Bloxwich 'Arry was gawping down her top.

Although she had been expecting Tony the Pizza and was slightly shocked to find it wasn't she knew who the unexpected visitors were, Jessie and One Arm Louis went back a long way, but as business acquaintances only, much to One Arm's regret.

Some quick thinking was in order.

"One Arm," she enthused, "welcome to our grow-your-own allotment party, you are the first of the guests to arrive….

What, no bottle of wine, didn't you know it is customary for the guests to bring either a bottle of wine or a bouquet of flowers for the hostess."

One Arm Louis hardly heard her, his attention was focused fully on Tony the Pizza….

Now let the fun begin…

One Arm barged past Jessie and forced his way into the hut.

"Don't say, 'excuse me,' will you?"

One Arm Louis wasn't listening.

"Come to collect, eh, Tony?"

Eli shot a look at Enoch, who shrugged, then at Jessie who held out her hands as if to say, don't ask me."

"Don't be shy, lad, how much have you copped for?"

Blank looks all round.

"Your pal the lawyer 'ere, 'as 'e read the Will yet? How much loot has your favourite aunt left you, Tony? Is she the one with the stop me and buy one ice-cream fortune? Has she left you enough to move up in the world….? Owning all those ice cream kiosks on every sea-front in England it should be…If so, my boy, social enhancement's not going to be at my expense, let me make that crystal… Unless thee can now afford a partnership…"

One Arm Louis bent over Eli/Louis to stress his words….
Wait a minute…there's something wrong, the zits are all in the wrong place an' this geezer has got them all over his nose!
"'Ere, yo ay Tony the Pizza!"

"I never said I was," whimpered Eli.

One Arm turned to Jessie, she couldn't help but notice he didn't look any too happy.

"No, One Arm, he ay Tony the Pizza… this is Eli Stone, a friend of mine, he works on the drains."

One Arm sat on the corner of the table.

"Not Tony the Pizza…?"

"No."

"Then what is this lawyer doing reading Tony the Pizza's aunt's Will?"

"I ay a lawyer, I'm a brickie," spluttered Enoch.

"Then yo ay qualified to read a Will, who the hell are you?"

"Enoch Stone, my brother's brother."

"Your brother's brother?"

Aye, 'im what's sat 'ere, 'im what looks as if he's gonna wet 'isself."

"And there ay no Will," added Jessie. She frowned, what Will?

One Arm looked back at Jessie. "So, there's no money from a newly snuffed it aunt for Tony the Pizza?"

Jessie shrugged, "don't think so, I would've 'eard."

Enoch stood, "fancy a cup of tea…er….?"

"This is One Arm Louis Ferrari, Enoch." Jessie smiled.

Enoch noticed that One Arm Louis had in fact two arms, each with a perfectly good hand on the end of each.

"E's got two arms," he whispered quietly to Jessie but obviously not quietly enough, One Arm heard him.

"Of course I've got two arms…"

Jessie stood between them, the last thing they needed now was One Arm Louis to give a demonstration.

"He is called One Arm Louis, Enoch because he has a habit of tearing off one arm from people he doesn't like."

"Whoops… any road, Mister One Arm" spluttered Enoch, "dust want a cup of tea? We've got condensed milk."

One Arm shook his head vigorously, Bloxwich 'Arry nodded, just as vigorously, but he was to be disappointed again.

One Arm was in danger of getting confused. He took a deep breath.

"Is it yo what's put the word out that Tony the Pizza would learn something to his advantage if he turned up at this hut at midnight tonight?"

Three heads nodded as one.

"Why?"

Jessie took over. "The secret groaty pudding recipe."

One Arm wasn't sure he could take much more of this.

"What secret groaty pudding recipe?"

She nodded. "Chugger Riley wants Tony so's he can get 'old of the secret groaty pudding recipe, Chugger wants it to be the highlight of a banquet in a few weeks' time – incidentally, yo'm invited."

One Arm scratched his neck, "Why would Tony the Pizza have this.. this.. secret groaty pudding recipe?"

"He hasn't." Jessie smiled again.

"But yo just said…."

She shook her head. "Tony the Pizza ay got it but Chugger reckons Tony con lead us to 'im what 'as."

"And who…?"

She smiled again, she was loving this, "thee…"

"Me?"

"Chugger says that yo' must 'ave the recipe as there's only the two of thee with the resources to pull off a heist as big as that and 'e needs the secret recipe for the banquet, so we were told we 'ad to trap Tony the Pizza and take 'im to Chugger so's 'e could get the exact whereabouts of the recipe out of 'im, where ever it is yo've 'id it, and as yo'r second in command Tony is bound to know."

It was silence for several seconds.

One Arm wiped the bread crumbs from his trousers as he stood up, he noticed how close he had been to getting a dollop of tomato sauce all over his arse.. Heads would have rolled…..

"The problem is, Jessie, I haven't a clue what you are talking about, I do not have the secret groaty pudding recipe… I have never had the secret groaty pudding recipe… why would I have the secret groaty pudding recipe…. I have never wanted the secret groaty pudding recipe."

"I day know there was a secret groaty pudding recipe," muttered Bloxwich 'Arry.

"But Chugger says it was thee who broke into Brierley Hill town hall, cracked the safe and stole it out of spite so that 'e cor put on the banquet! Like 'e says there's only yo and 'im what could 'ave done it and it wor 'im, so it must be thee!"

One Arm slowly shook his head.

"Sorry, Jessie, just for once, I'm not guilty."

"Chugger is going to love this!" Jessie collapsed back onto the sofa, she didn't care that four pairs of eyes were glued to her legs.

One Arm was staring intently at Eli. "Yo'm a spitting image…"

Jessie nodded, "we know, that's what caused all this in the first place, me mistakin' Eli for Tony and blabbing to Chugger.

Eli was shocked, "It was thee was it, well thanks a bunch, Jessie, I love you to."

"I'm sorry, Eli, them gas lamps doe give off a lot of light, it was a simple mistake an' yo am the spittin' image, so it ay all my fault."

She turned back to One Arm Louis, "Any road, Chugger is convinced that Eli is Tony the Pizza which is why we 'ave to get 'old of the real Tony to get Eli off the 'ook with Chugger…… So that's why we'm 'ere waiting for midnight and a visit from the real Tony the Pizza." stressed Jessie, just in case there was any doubt, Black Country hoodlums were notorious for being thick, "Eli and Enoch put the word all round town for Tony to be 'ere at midnight."

"To hear something to his advantage, I know," muttered One Arm. "Except Tony has been in Cheltenham all day so he won't have heard so he won't be coming."

One Arm's fertile if diseased brain was ticking over in a very productive manner….

"No, Eli, yo' ay Tony the Pizza, but if we can keep Chugger Riley thinking yo am, at least for a while, we might turn this to our advantage."

"To our advantage, One Arm?" queried Jessie.

"Well… Mine."

That's more like it.

"When Tony gets back I'll tell 'im to get lost for a day or two and Eli here can take his place."

Eli was appalled, "I doe want to be a gangster!"

Hardly that," chuckled One Arm, "but as far as Chugger Riley is concerned you are going to be."

One Arm paced around the hut a while, no-one dared move. "Right… this is what we, I mean you, Tony, are going to do."

"He means you, Eli," Jessie wasn't confident.

Counterfeit Tony the Pizza

One Arm outlined his plan. Eli in the guise of Tony the Pizza was to innocently walk into the trap laid by Chugger Riley, he was then, after a slight delay - he had to put up a show of loyalty for One Arm Louis in order to convince Chugger he was genuine – he will confess that he knows the location of the secret groaty pudding recipe – as given to him by his boss the aforesaid One Arm Louis Ferrari.

This location he would reluctantly tell Chugger about, on condition that he was allowed to go free before Chugger raided the secret hiding place, he was still a loyal member of One Arm Louis' gang and as such didn't want Chugger to drop him in the clart.

According to One Arm, Chugger would agree, he has no argument as such with Tony the Pizza and certainly wouldn't want any undue friction, not if he was to lord it over all the other local gangsters at the banquet, one of whom would be Tony's boss One Arm Louis.

Eli tentatively raised one arm, "What if he doesn't agree, Chugger Riley, I mean?"

One Arm shrugged, "then I'll send Bloxwich 'Arry down the canal with a boathook."

"What for?" Eli asked but had a feeling he knew the answer.

"To pull your corpse out before it pollutes the water."

Eli was right, he did know the answer; being a gangster – if only a temporary gangster - wasn't going to be all beer and skittles.

Do you know what, thought Jessie, off the top of his head that's not a bad plan, in fact it's a bloody good plan, maybe I should align myself to One Arm Louis, after all years ago I was his favourite waitress for a while before my own 'business' took off when he had that caff by the canal, so why not again, well, not as a waitress maybe? What has Chugger Riley ever done for me, except promise to do me a mischief for fingering the wrong Tony the Pizza? It's a no-brainer, really.

Jessie's brain was on overdrive….

Yes, she thought, it is time to suck up to my potential new boy-friend, I could be his new housekeeper at his private apartment - providing we can keep his old lady in the dark, including about the apartment of which she didn't even knew it existed.

"I don't know how you do it, One Arm, that is a stroke of genius and as quick as a flash, like I say I don't know how you do it."

Bloxwich 'Arry was actually applauding.

"Glad you like it, Jessie, is it a good plan do you reckon?"

"Like I said – boss – a stroke of genius."

"Jessie's casual use of the word *boss* was not lost on One Arm Louis.

He answered her smile with one of his own, actually it came out more like a sneer but he did his best.

"I'll tell you what, Jessie, while we wait for Tony here to ingratiate himself with Chugger Riley why don't you and I spend a little time together over a couple of bottles of brown ale at my private apartment" – the aforesaid private apartment, the very one where Jessie harboured ambitions – "overlooking the canal, the views at this time of year are spectacular."

But not half as spectacular as the view I hope to get, he thought. He shuddered…. those legs.

Jessie knew the score, she also knew that her strategic use of the word 'boss' had done the trick: this was a heaven sent opportunity to work on her audition for the position of housekeeper; it was also going to cost him more than a bottle of brown ale, what he had in mind was worth at least a bottle of bubbly.

"I can't wait."

That was it, job done, at least for the moment. Eli, in the guise of Tony the Pizza would lead Chugger Riley to the secret location of the bogus secret recipe while Jessie allowed One Arm to explore her secret locations, secret at least from the paying punters, One Arm was a friend, that was different.

"What about me, what do I do while the rest of you are either playing cowboys and Indians or partaking of a little hanky panky?" queried Enoch.

"You play Tony the Pizza's wing-man," to One Arm Louis it was obvious.

"Wing man, what's a wing man?"

Jessie sighed, she wasn't used to dealing with civilians.

"You watch his back, a kind of bodyguard, you look after 'im if the going gets tough."

Enoch wished he'd never asked. "That boathook's gonna be busy."

The meeting broke up, Jessie would go back to One Arm's luxury apartment, and a bottle of bubbly or several - or else severe disappointment, and it wouldn't be hers – relieved she didn't have to spend another night on that disgusting sofa, she could swear there was something moving around inside it in the middle of the night; Enoch back to his good lady to tell her he had finished sowing the soon to be prize-winning sweet peas, and to tell her the prize money might be enough for a luxury weekend away in the Robin Hood caravan park at Rhyl, 'nothing is too much for you my sweet, even staying up all night in that freezing cold shed with only a cup of tea for company' - prior to sneaking off to take up his new role as bodyguard to a look-a-like gangster just in case One Arm's master plan turns to crap, while Bloxwich 'Arry would be going back to bed on his rented canal boat to hopefully dream about Jessie's delightful assets, then first thing in the morning he would go round all the canal bank sheds – the ones where the owners were still in bed of course - and try to nick a boathook.

Eli meanwhile for the rest of the night, what was left of it, would have the longest panic attack ever known to mankind prior to his knocking on the door of Chugger Riley's private suite at The Continental early the following morning.

Am yo looking for me?

The housekeeper, by the name Elise answered the door of Chugger Riley's private apartment on the top floor of what used to be a warehouse but was now with no taste whatsoever a loft conversion over his club. Elise was dressed for work, she bent down to pick up the morning newspaper making sure the visitor had a good view, the visitor felt faint.

Elise smiled, the view is for nothing, she could have said, but to explore costs more than you can afford.

"Can I help you?" she enquired, unfortunately her voice was less than sophisticated.

Eli managed to control his breathing, the anxiety of having to be here added to Elise's bold front was almost too much for his delicate heart.

"Would'st tell Mister Riley he wants to see me."

"Pardon…?

"Mister Riley wishes to see me, will yo go and tell 'im?"

She didn't move from the spot, she turned and with the energy of a canal boat hooter she bawled along the corridor.

"Chugger, there's a geezer 'er what wants to see thee."

Eli shook his head, "no I doe, it's Chugger what wants to see me!"

The foghorn started up again, "'E cor meck 'is mind up, 'e says it ay 'im what wants to see thee it's thee what wants to see 'im!"

A large and imposing figure appeared at the end of the corridor, it was dressed in an all-over Chinese affair belted at the waist, its feet were adorned in silk slippers and believe it or not one eye held a monocle. The apparition slid across the wall-to-wall hand embroidered and very expensive Egyptian carpet – predominantly blue, Chugger's favourite colour and came to rest a feet away from Eli, all the while the eyes appraising the visitor, taking particular notice of the possibility of a bulge under an armpit the sure sign of a concealed weapon.

As Eli was straight up and straight down and almost disappeared completely when he turned sideways that worry was soon dispelled.

"Well?" That was it, no 'how do you do', no 'good morning how can I help you?'... Just "well?"

Eli tried to look a shade nonchalant... "The word is yo want a word wi' me."

"Who exactly is me?"

Eli pushed out his chest, there was hardly a noticeable difference.

"Tony, Tony the Pizza, top torpedo for One Arm Louis Ferrari."

"Aaaagh...Come in, Tony, my home is your home...Any friend of One Arm Louis is a friend of mine, make yourself at home..." Chugger placed his hand on Elise's shoulder 'accidentally' pulling down a shoulder strap, she giggled but didn't put it back, "anything you want you only have to ask.. eh, Elise?"

The housekeeper stood to one side allowing Eli to cross the threshold, he tried to squeeze by without making physical contact but she made sure he failed... Elise smiled, her boss's wish was hers to obey.

The visitor was ushered in to a large and luxuriously furnished sitting room, the housekeeper indicated that Eli was to sit in one of the large cushion strewn sofas, so he did. Chugger whispered in Elise's ear.

"Look after our visitor Elise while I get dressed," Chugger chuckled and slid out of the room, Elise smiled again.

Under Chugger's whispered instructions she was to try to extract the location of the secret recipe from Tony using any method she saw fit, if she failed then Chugger would try more drastic methods.... But, it was her turn first.

She studied her victim, what a specimen, all string and paper, how was he the main man in One Arm's gang?

She played with the wanton shoulder strap, sat and crossed her legs.

Not a patch on Jessie's legs thought Eli, quite unmoved.

The other shoulder strap had to go which almost caused free-fall but there was no re-action from the idiot sitting facing her, either he was suffering from the after-effects of a serious operation on his manhood or he was bent.

She should have taken into account that he was terrified - partly of the situation in which he found himself, but mainly of her.

Keep trying... Chugger's orders.

"What can I offer you, Tony, Chugger will be ages yet, he takes ages getting dressed, so I think we might have time for whatever you fancy," Elise laughed, the laugh came out of her bright red rimmed mouth with a raucous cackle that would have guaranteed her a part as a witch in Macbeth.

Eli tried to laugh but couldn't, it wasn't easy to laugh when you are trying not to wet your trousers.

Look at him, what am I supposed to do with that?

She shook her head and pulled up her shoulder straps.

"Relax, Tony, I'm only jokin', the bit of whatever you fancy I have in mind comes in a mug and it's called coffee or tea."

She was beaten and she knew it.

Eli relaxed a little, although he couldn't believe what was happening to him; all his adult life he had only ever been asked to cope with one woman, his missus, and after the honeymoon he had even begun to like the arrangement but now there was Jessie with those legs and now this new one with the impressive double frontage and his nerves were at breaking point.

Elise poured two cups of a brown liquid which turned out to be coffee out of a silver coffee pot and passed one cup to Eli, he didn't know whether to tip some of the coffee into the saucer which was his normal way of drinking tea or coffee but decided not to, these people may not be familiar with the traditional ways of the Black Country male.

"White sugar or brown, Tony?"

"Neither ta love, ast got any condensed milk?"

Further conversation or even further attempts of seduction had Elise decided to have another go were prevented by the return of Chugger Riley, he had rushed through his ablutions; now that he had met him his instincts had told him that Tony the Pizza was never going to fall for Elise's charms, he looked to be far too sophisticated – Eli's missus would have laughed her socks off is she had heard that - but this meeting with One Arm's top torpedo was far too important to risk the visitor saying he wasn't going to wait and go buggering off...

"Tony," he enthused, "has Elise given you what you want?" From the corner of his eye he saw Elise slowly shaking her head. I was right, he thought, either that or Elise is losing her touch.

" Ah, I see she has, coffee, sorry we don't have any condensed milk, I know how you guys from the other side of the canal like your condensed milk,"

He must have been listening at the door.

Chugger smiled a syrupy smooth smile and sat on a large armchair opposite Eli, not once taking his eyes off his visitor.

Chugger cut directly to the chase; don't give your man the opportunity to settle down and definitely don't give him the time to come up with any bullshit.

"I haven't time to waste, my friend, I have a business to run, canal boat schedules to work out, recipes for the restaurant to finalise, girls to interview for the strip club...... so...The secret groaty pudding recipe?"

No response as arranged, Jessie had told Eli to make Chugger wait, don't give him the information too easy he might get suspicious.

"The secret groaty pudding recipe," repeated Chugger, maybe there was a hint of a little more urgency in his voice?

Once again Eli ignored the request, if request it was, so far it had been no more than a mention.

"Don't play with me Tony, you know why I wanted to see thee, I want the secret groaty pudding recipe, and I know your boss has it, and I also know that you are the only member of the gang who would also know, One Arm trusts you, as a back-up in case anything should happen to him - which could be arranged if necessary – so logic dictates he will have told you where it is, so don't mess with me, you know I am right."

Eli wanted to un-cross his legs, the left one was going to sleep, but he decided against it, any undue movement in the lower quarters might prove disastrous.

"Ast got any more coffee, Elise love, that's a tasty brew yo've got there?" Eli was amazed at his own bravado.

Chugger sent the coffee pot spinning across the room,

"Bugger the coffee, you scrawny little scroat, I want the secret groaty pudding recipe and I know you know where it is!"

Eli was shaking in his boots, was now the time to give in?

"What if I dun, what's it to thee, and I ay scrawny, my missus says I'm a lean mean fighting machine."

Actually she has never said anything of the sort, all she has ever done is complain that no matter how much food she stuffs into him he still looks like a five foot six inch well-worn garden rake with zits.

"I want the recipe Tony and I doe care how I gets it, if I 'ave to I'll tear you limb from limb and post your body parts back to One Arm Louis with my compliments at the same time as I send him his invitation to my mayoral banquet….."

Chugger calmed down, a bad sign…

"Where is the recipe, Tony? Be a good boy and tell Uncle Chugger."

Eli looked across to a clock on the mantle shelf.

"Good grief, is that the time, I have to go, it's been nice meeting you, Mr Riley, and you Elise."

The problem was he couldn't get out of the sofa it was so large and sumptuous it was trying to eat him.

"Let me make it clear, Mister Pizza, the only way you go out of here without giving me the location of the secret groaty pudding recipe it will be in a box marked 'Made in England, genuine oak, rest in peace' – mind you, I'll do you proud, it'll have real brass handles, no rubbish from Chugger Riley – I always keep one or two in stock, you never know when you might need one; then when your boss One Arm Louis Ferrari comes to my banquet he will be presented with the bill – mates rates of course - for your funeral… Do I make myself clear, young man?"

Eli calculated that now would be the time to give in and tell his host what he wanted to know before Chugger measured him up to decide which coffin he would be stuffed in. And even if this isn't the time it would have to do, he didn't think he could wait – toilet-wise – for much longer.

"Okay… Okay… I'll tell thee, it's no skin off my nose, on condition that One Arm never gets to know I've told thee where it is."

Chugger nodded, "Agreed, and very sensible if may say so."

Business was conducted in a civilised manner, Eli wrote out the secret location of the secret recipe on Elise's pinny, she in turn provided tuna sandwiches and the promise of an interesting night out any time 'Tony' wanted and mine genial host promised that Tony the Pizza could have a job working for Chugger Riley Enterprises any time he wanted to leave One Arm Louis Ferrari.

Ten minutes later the deed was done and Eli cum Tony was free to go.

Elise helped him out of the chair, he could see that far down her top he thought he caught a glimpse of her shoes.

He hesitated…

"There is just one thing…"

Chugger held out his arms, "Anything, Tony…"

"Can I use your toilet?"

A successful outcome

They – meaning Eli, Enoch and Jessie - met in the garden at One Arm's luxury pad, servants bustled around, tea and cakes were the thing.

One Arm Louis was as pleased as punch, his 'new' Tony the Pizza had come up trumps, his sworn enemy Chugger Riley was soon to receive his comeuppance courtesy of a perfectly ordinary groaty pudding recipe as written out by Jessie, but as Chugger was hardly a home-cook he wouldn't notice the difference, and his renowned and well-advertised mayoral banquet would be an abject failure once his well-heeled guests discovered that the 'secret' groaty pudding they had devoured with admirable gusto at forty quid a throw – proceeds to a charity nominated by Chugger Riley - was available at every caff in the Black Country for a tanner a portion….

A plateful of cream doughnuts seemed a small price to pay.

"He didn't argue when you told him where he could find the recipe?"

"Nope, he just rubbed his hands together and giggled."

It couldn't have gone better.

The Chugger Riley Expedition

Chugger wasted no time, the mayoral banquet was now only a couple of weeks away and there was no time to lose. He picked four of his best men, made sure they were armed and at precisely eight o'clock on the morning of Saturday the ninth they set off on their quest. It was going to be a long day, it was at least a five hour drive followed by a boat ride to the island. Why in hell's name One Arm chose to bury the secret groaty pudding recipe on an island off the coast of North Wales was a mystery to Chugger; from Tipton to Stourbridge on a canal boat was one thing but half an hour or more on a run-down old fishing boat in stormy weather on the Irish sea was something else.

There is little point in relating the journey, suffice to say that it was almost dark when they reached the cottage where the fishing boat and its owner should be found.

Yes, as arranged he was there, the boat was ready, plenty of fuel and sick bags a-plenty, the fisherman in question knew how these English hated the sea.

The two cars were parked out of sight in the barn and as the sun set over the island which stood out like a black stain against the reddening sky the little boat was pushed off the beach, then pointing in the right direction put-putted its way across the sound to the island.

All we need say about the journey by boat is it's a good job there were plenty of sick bags.

The boat scraped its bottom on the sand on the only inlet big enough to land a boat.

They couldn't wait to get off it and onto solid ground.

The fisherman/ boat owner was instructed to stay with the boat, under no circumstances was he to leave without them, or worse follow them.

Being a good capitalist he settled down in the back of the boat, wrapped an old army blanket over him, opened a bottle of whisky and prepared to give his clients the bad news, if he didn't get his money here and now they would have to swim back to the mainland.

Now it was up to Chugger… Who couldn't read a map to save his life, never mind follow hand-written instructions done by someone whose only claim to fame writing-wise was filling in betting slips.

Eli's written instructions were fairly comprehensive verging on the impossible – 'from the beach follow the track up the hill until you get to the gate, turn right through the gate, close the gate behind you to keep the cows in, mind the cowpats, at the end of this track you will see a small corrugated shed used for cattle feed, this is your destination.'

It sounds easy enough.

'If the bull is in residence' maybe not so easy – 'you will have to entice him out before attempting to dig but using the pantomime cow suit hanging from a hook behind the door this should be easy, but make sure that the man in the back end of the cow suit protects his rear from intruders.'

The bull was missing – as Eli predicted it probably would be – there was a herd of Friesian cows in the field, what would a bull want with an lonely empty barn on a moonlit night when he could take a short stroll in the field and stay there for heifer and heifer; sighs of relief all round, especially from the man who having drawn the short straw had been destined to be the arse end of the cow.

Completely out of breath they reached the corrugated shed; that's the advantage of working on the canal, there aren't any hills.

Giving his troops a five minute breather Chugger consulted Eli's written instructions.

'Under the old tractor tyre you will find dumped in the corner of the shed dig down a foot, scrape the soil away carefully because there you will find a Midland Counties milk bottle, and we don't want you breaking it and getting an ouchy on your pinky; inside the bottle you will see a rolled up piece of paper. When you have done this you will have found the secret hiding place of the secret groaty pudding recipe. Place said secret groaty pudding recipe in a zip-up water-proof pocket for safekeeping.

Re-trace your steps back to the boat and get the hell out of there before the bull returns for a well-earned kip...'

Which is exactly what they did, the tractor tyre was dragged out of the way, using the spade provided they took it in turns to dig, one digging, two watching in the grand tradition of the Great British working male and one on watch, not for the foreman, for the bull.

And there it was.

"Found it," breathed one of the men, "right where Tony said it would be."

Chugger, on bended knees, never mind the arthritis this was too important to worry about the odd twinge, retrieved the Midland Counties milk bottle with all the reverence needed for such an occasion. The secret groaty pudding recipe was his..... The mayoral banquet would be a resounding success, another step towards being selected as prospective parliamentary candidate for the next general election.. Anyone who could produce groaty pudding at a banquet made from the ancient secret recipe deserves the nomination at least, if not automatic selection.

The little group made its way back to the beach, no man dared to speak it was such a solemn moment.

The owner of the fishing boat, in the best traditions of a North Wales fisherman held out his hand for his fee, Chugger was so delighted to have the secret recipe in his zip-up waterproof pocket he not only handed over the agreed fee but a little bit extra, enough for a bottle of whisky..

Chugger didn't come down to earth until the car pulled up outside the club on the canal bank, such was his euphoria. With the promise of a bonus he dismissed his men.
Elise came to the door of his private apartment to meet him, he patted the trouser pocket holding the secret recipe but she mis-interpreted where he was patting and took off her skirt.

The Mayoral Banquet

One Arm Louis received the news almost at once, Chugger's expedition to wild Wales had been a success, the secret recipe was now safely tucked away in the safe in Chugger's office, the next time it would see the light of day would be when the chef asked for it so that he could prepare the main dish of the banquet, groaty pudding made to the secret recipe.
The whole affair was guaranteed to be a resounding success. Eli and Enoch had accepted an invitation to afternoon tea at One Arm's apartment, they were met by Jessie, radiant and satisfied with her new lot in life.
It was a civilised affair, two different flavours of tea, a plateful of scones each and lashings of blackcurrant jam. Lovely.
"Am yo goin' to sabotage Chugger Riley's banquet, One Arm?" asked Enoch, between scones.
One Arm Louis shook his head, "no, my friend I am going to do nothing. The impending disaster will in no way be connected to my good-self, as far as I am concerned, the banquet will be a rip-roaring success."
"The impending disaster…?" Eli frowned.
"Oh yes," One Arm Louis smiled. "the impending disaster…. with absolutely no banquetorial sabotage by myself or indeed by anyone whatsoever as far as I am aware."
They didn't understand.

One Arm's new girlfriend smiled, she wasn't really listening, she was bathing in the new-found comfort she had never experienced in her previous life.

Josie could have the tenancy of the gas lamp as a free gift, the young lady sitting crossed legged opposite Enoch giving him palpitations wouldn't need it again, not whilst under the protection of One Arm Louis…

"Pour the drinks, Jessie love," instructed One Arm.

Jessie smiled and uncrossed her legs, Enoch nearly fainted; Eli smiled enigmatically, he and he alone knew that Jessie had called round to the house the previous evening to thank him for helping her leave the mean streets of Tipton and fall into the protective and sumptuous custody of One Arm Louis Ferrari. Her thank you knew no bounds. As a PS she added that what he had just received may have been a well-earned thank you but that was it, any further favours and he would have to pay – mates rates of course to include a substantial discount.

That wonderful evening had been followed with the devastating news that was delivered in the next morning's post that his missus wouldn't be coming home, she was staying at her mother's for good, she had left him, meaning that Eli's last twenty four hours had gone from brilliant to bloody fantastic.

The great day arrived, the great and the good spent hours preparing themselves, the ultimate aim of course was to make an impression and lord it over their so-called friends, they arrived in their droves, limousines and bored looking chauffeurs filled all the available nooks and crannies along the canal bank, the occupants disembarked in the manner they had been taught, heads high, legs together: men in monkey suits flaunting gold watch chains and monogrammed cufflinks, the ladies in every bit of crappy but expensive looking jewellery they owned, powdered cleavages threatening to burst out of

49

low-cut gowns and every over emblem to bad taste you can think of; fur coat and no knickers most of them but they made a fine spectacle.

It was drinky-poos in the private members lounge to start, most of them, even the fully paid-up - without the wife's knowledge - members of the strip club had never been in this room, did it occur to any of them that it was their money that had paid for it? Of course not, but this and the golf club fees were an unavoidable major and oft-times crippling expense, social climbing is an expensive but very necessary business.

The Mayor expressed his approval of the surroundings just as if he had never been in the place, even though he spends every Friday evening in there entertained by young ladies of the very lowest repute.

The Mayoress kept her mouth firmly shut, best not to mention that she noticed the curtains were new – and they matched Chugger's pyjamas, how novel.

Chugger was lording it above everyone, this was his day, he had planned this event right down to the last detail and if it didn't immediately elevate him to parliamentary candidate for the '"I've got everything, so screw you' party at the next general election nothing would.

One Arm Louis, with Jessie on his arm arrived politely late, but just in time to partake of the pre-dinner drinkies.

The two men shook hands and Chugger welcomed his rival to the party. Not a mention was made of the on-going feud between the two gangsters, a mention of the secret groaty pudding recipe would be very infra dig, Business was business maybe, but tonight was for enjoyment, the war could be put on hold until the morrow.

Jessie was breathless and a bag of nerves, not because of the amorous activities she had enjoyed with her new boyfriend prior to this wonderful night out – the gas lamp was already a fading memory - but more because she believed she was a Cinderella figure way out of her depth in the company of these upper crust women who she thought were not only more expensively dressed and dripping with sparklers but far more respectable than she.

She was jealous, it was as simple as that… One Arm noticed and vowed to spill the beans to her later, especially about My Lady Mayoress.

In his own way One Arm was proud of Jessie, her past he didn't care about, everybody had a past, no-one worse than he and the fact that Chugger was throwing the looks that could kill their way was a double satisfaction.

"Have you met my new girlfriend, Chugger? Of course you must have, but let me introduce her in case you have forgotten who she is….

How could he forget… the tramp… but, no, no bad mouthing tonight…

"Hello, Jessie, may I say how beautiful you look…"

She curtsied, head high, body straight, no free looks down her sequined strapless top for him, although she did flutter her eyelashes.

 A nice touch, thought One Arm.

"Well, how very kind of you, sir, it's nice of you to say so…"

The Mayoress was looking daggers.

The Master of Ceremonies banged his gold plated gavel.

"Dinner is served," his frilly cuffs managed to hide his calloused hands and dirty finger nails, only an hour before he had been shovelling coal on to a canal boat destined for Wolverhampton, but having been selected by Chugger from all the other wannabe MC applicants and was getting an extra ten bob for his trouble he was determined to do a professional job.

And so it came to pass… The grand banquet began, Chugger was almost wetting himself with the excitement, this was the culmination of years of strife, graft, thuggery and theft.

It was time….. The groaty pudding made to the secret groaty pudding recipe 'rescued' from an island off the North Wales coast made its grand entrance, soaked in brandy and well-alight in the manner of a plum pudding making its triumphant entrance in the middle class homes of England at Christmas-time , except this particular silver platter groaning with the weight of the groaty pudding was piped in by three penny whistles and a kazoo, playing 'Onward Christian Soldiers' - which were according to Chugger, who had been told this by a gypsy, the traditional musical instruments of the canal people, although why 'Onward Christian Soldiers' the gypsy hadn't explained, only that he had a lot of sympathy for the Salvation Army.

The highly trained waiters and waitresses approached, it was now their job to serve. Chugger had decided not to use his own staff, the serving of the groaty pudding was to be as good as it gets so he had employed agency staff, qualified and slick. Soon every guest was staring at a genuine Royal Worcester plate and on each plate was a generous serving of groaty pudding, the steam rising to the ceiling.

The Master of Ceremonies gently tapped a silver spoon on the side of a Stourbridge cut glass goblet, the room went quiet. Yes, as with the Royal Worcester, all the cut glass decanters goblets and assorted glassware had been liberated from rival canal boats.

To rapturous applause, Chugger stood and bathed in his success. This moment was the culmination of many years dreaming and scheming.

"Lord Mayor, my Lady Mayoress (The Mayoress blushed) ladies and gentlemen, it gives me great pleasure to look down upon you; here we all are gathered together to savour the delights of our beloved Black Country, in front of you is a dish so delicate the recipe is a well-guarded secret, later we shall drink in the aroma of genuine Black Country stout or brown ale, with barley wine for the ladies, but to compliment the delicate flavour of the groaty pudding we will accompany it with the time-honoured drink of all canal boat people, Bank's Mild…. Enjoy."

To even more rapturous applause Chugger sat, his cheeks flushed with success.

Taking their cue from Chugger the congregation picked up their silver forks and dug in… Most of them had spent their childhood raised on groaty pudding, although it would be a surprise if any would admit it… But this was no ordinary groaty pudding – not at forty quid a throw - this was groaty pudding made to a secret recipe known only to a handful of people most of whom were now under the sod – and now Chugger Riley and his chef 'Billy the Chip' of course.

Chugger's disappointment.

"If I understand you correctly, Mister Ferrari…" Eli was still uncomfortable calling his new employer 'One Arm'.

Oh yes, new employer indeed, Eli had been offered and had accepted a position in the organisation. He was to skipper his own boat carrying general cargo but specialising in barrels of mushy peas down to Bristol on their way to America where apparently mushy peas are a great delicacy. Eli's new boat had comfortable living accommodation and room for a passenger if he so wished. Jessie noticed this and thought, yes, why not, the occasional trip down the canal might prove to be an aid to the complexion…. Being forced to share the confines of the neat but cramped cabin with Eli never even crossed her mind.

"If I understand you correct, Mister Ferrari you got Jessie to write out the recipe – a very ordinary recipe – knowing that Chugger wouldn't notice there was nothing secret about it and then you got your boys to hide it on the island…..Which means I take it you have the secret recipe hidden away safe?"

One Arm shook his head, "No, I am afraid not, no-one seems to know where the secret groaty pudding recipe is I am sorry to say, it was certainly stolen on the night of the burglary and it would be worth a fortune on the open market, in fact everyone is surprised it has never been offered for sale, the vendor would be able to retire on the proceeds, although I suppose rather like a work of art, the Mona Lisa or whatever a buyer would be difficult to find, its possession could never be made public, the outcry would be catastrophic. Chugger believed the perpetrator to be me and I confess to believing at that time that it had been nicked by Chugger…But, as it turns out it was neither of us.

Enoch giggled. "Are you saying that Chugger charged his guests forty quid a throw to nosh on a perfectly ordinary plateful of groaty pudding that the rest of us can buy for a tanner in any high street?"

One Arm smiled. "How sad."

"He's not going to like it," warned Jessie.

One Arm smiled, "that was the idea, my love."

Why did Eli feel a tinge of jealousy when One Arm called Jessie 'my love'?

"He'll be livid when he finds out it wasn't made to the secret recipe," Jessie was shaking her head.

"He might not find out, why should he find out?" Enoch was frowning, "the banquet was last week, why should any of his guests find out it was all a scam, admittedly an un-intentional scam on the part of Chugger, the groaty pudding was eaten, the recipe is now locked away in Chugger's safe, he won't even bother to look at it."

One Arm chuckled, "Oh, they will find out it was a scam, and unfortunately Chugger will get the blame."

It was Jessie's turn to frown, "and I guess that when they find out it was a scam they will have you to thank?"

"Well…. If they knew it was me, yes, I suppose so, but they will never find out it was me, do I make myself clear?"

"Yes, boss," they uttered in unison.

At pretty much the same time as this cosy gathering was indulging in tea and cakes Chugger Riley was receiving a visitor, Elise showed the visitor up to the private apartment where he was asked to wait a moment whilst she fetched her employer.

"Who is it, Elise?" Chugger was expecting yet another one of his banqueting guests to thank him for a perfectly lovely evening, if he was lucky it would be a grateful woman.

"Chief Superintendent Watkins apparently… And he is in uniform."

Come to enquire why he wasn't invited, I expect thought Chugger, he wasn't worried.

He breezed into the room without a care in the world, quite prepared to invite the chief Super next time in exchange for .? Well… he would think of something.

The Chief Superintendent rose, he had heard about the sofa so he had sat on an upright dining chair.

With no pre-amble whatsoever….

"Elias Ebenezer Riley, aka Chugger, I am arresting you on suspicion of breaking and entering the Mayoral office and the removal of one item, too wit, the groaty pudding recipe that you believe to be an age-old secret handed down from father to son over many generations."

Chugger was thrown off-balance.

"I don't have to believe it, it was the secret groaty pudding recipe…."

"Ah, so you admit it!"

The game was up, Chugger was caught groaty-handed as it were.

With a sigh he reached into his ornate Victorian roll-top desk and extracted the key to the safe which he handed to the Chief Super.

With some ceremony the policeman opened the safe and extracted the reason for Chugger's evident distress.

The chief Superintendent reverently unfolded the paper and read the scrawl – Jessie was always being told off at school for her lousy writing.

After a moment or two the Chief Super faced Chugger, he wasn't smiling. "What the hell is this?"

"You know what it is, it's the secret groaty pudding recipe, it's a fair cop, cop."

The Chief Super found this funny, Chugger didn't understand why.

"The hell it is, it is exactly what my informant said I would find, I have to say I wasn't inclined to believe him – or her – but now…." He waved the paper under Chugger's nose..

"So, what are you trying to pull, my son?"

Chugger felt uneasy, the Chief Super explained.

"This, my son, is the recipe for a perfectly ordinary groaty pudding, there is nothing secret about it, when my missus has an attack of the croup I cook her this all the time…. Not only that but groaty pudding to this exact recipe is on sale in every high street this side of Birmingham for a tanner a throw…..

And if it is supposed to be an age-old recipe written back in the dark ages or whenever how come it is scrawled all over a brand-new sheet of paper torn from a Basildon Bond writing pad? Whoever wrote this couldn't even keep the words between the lines!"

Strangely he started laughing. "Is this what you were passing off as the secret groaty pudding at forty quid a plate?"

He couldn't stop laughing, "Wait until your illustrious guests find out, your life won't be worth a tanner never mind forty quid… The Mayor is going to love this – not."

Chugger snatched at the paper and held it up to the light, this sneering cop was right, the watermark was plain enough, it was 'Balsidon Bond' right enough….

"You had best come with me, Chugger, we can continue this conversation down the station, there is still the matter of a wrecked safe… and unlawful breaking and entering specifically to nick…" he had to stop for a second, he was laughing so much, "specifically to nick…this…the secret groaty pudding recipe!"

As they were going through the door, "You'd better tell me what you did with the mayoral chain while we are at it, 'cos that went walkabout at the same time…"

Chugger just looked blank.

"Never mind, Mister Riley, this should look good in court, master criminal nicked for the illegal possession of a sheet of Basildon Bond writing paper." He burst out laughing again.

In no time at all Chuggers's humiliation was complete, met in the street having paid his own bail by the Mayor he was politely informed that the best he could hope for wouldn't be as parliamentary candidate but as front-runner for the thieving barmpot of the year award.

Of course, not all the great and the good agreed with the Mayor, it was his worship after all who had been top dog at the banquet and therefore had taken most of the flack from other councillors – for which forty quid was considered cheap - eager to cash in on the Mayor's humiliation.. The Mayoress for example had thought it a good gag, money had been raised for charity from people who without the press publicity and the guaranteed picture in the newspaper turning up in all their finery for the banquet would never in million years put their hands in their pockets to help anybody, neither would they be seen to ask for their money back and thus be branded as a skinflint. – as the Mayoress was at pains to point out to Chugger at their very next private meeting at the club.

"So, no-one has any idea who nicked the secret recipe?" mused Jessie as she snuggled up to One Arm, whilst thinking about Eli and their forthcoming trip to Bristol – whilst Jessie was visiting her sick mother in Sutton Coldfield according to the story she had told One Arm Louis – her mother would fall sick with remarkable regularity from now on - but there we are, we are all entitled to a little excitement in our lives, although Eli coupled with excitement? That does sort of push the boundaries of credibility somewhat.

Yes, Jessie could count herself happy, not once did she have a pang of conscience about abandoning her gas lamp.

Finally

A new item on the menu, Groaty pudding suddenly appeared at a take-a-way shop on Brierley Hill high street a few months later, and according to its customers – of which there are many and still growing - the groaty pudding it sold was just that little bit more special than the groaty pudding to be found on every other high street....

The compliments flew thick and fast, much to the satisfaction of Abigail Hill, the mother of Brierley Hill town clerk, Lizzie Hill..... she who found the safe open on that fateful morning. No, Lizzie didn't hide it down her bra....

The truth was the secret groaty pudding recipe was never in the safe, in fact contrary to what the Mayor had told the police it had never been in the safe, it had lain quiet and forgotten in the top drawer of the town clerk's desk. She had been instructed by the Mayor to put it in the safe but she, perhaps flustered after returning from Councillor Hardcastle's office had simply forgotten all about it, until one day when she was leaving her employment having fallen rather too much for her councillor's charms and it was beginning to show and was cleaning out her desk she came across it and decided that perhaps her mother might be able to do something with it.

All that drama ending in a disappointing anti-climax – as Jessie might say after a night in the canal boat cabin with Eli.

The Enoch and Eli Trilogy

Carrying on with

The Strange Affair of the Great Mushy Peas Battle

Peter Yates

Things calmed down for a while, Chugger nursed his wounds, as he suspected he didn't receive the nomination for prospective parliamentary candidate it went to the captain of the golf club – a golf club owned by Chugger himself so that enhanced the humiliation - but he did have other things to think about and to take out his anger on his social climbing hitting a temporary brick wall his thoughts on these things were twenty four hours a day…. His revenge on One Arm Louis Ferrari for one thing, firstly for dropping him in the clart regarding the stolen mayoral chain with the police, a crime he hadn't committed and knew nothing about but was nevertheless still on bail for - and secondly for pinching one of his best girls, Jessie. As for Tony the Pizza he had yet to receive his just reward for sending Chugger on a wild recipe chase bobbing about all over the Irish sea.
The secret groaty pudding recipe was something else, Chugger would get over the being dropped in the you-know-what regarding the mayoral chain, he would get off the hook for that even if it meant encouraging someone else to confess, although even that might not be necessary, the police had failed to recover the mayoral chain and without the evidence they would find it hard to get a conviction – according to Chugger's solicitor; maybe even get over losing Jessie, she wasn't the only beautiful girl from whom he took a commission, but it would not be easy to get over being made a

fool of regarding the groaty pudding fiasco at the Mayoral banquet, not before handing out dire and excessive retribution. Eli started his new job, he loved it. Instead of spending his working life with his head stuck down a drain he was standing in the stern of his very own canal boat – well, maybe not exactly his own but when he went to work these days he had to make his own decisions so it felt like it was his boat – breathing in fresh country air; even the air in Tipton docks was an improvement to the fetid gas-ridden stuff he had previously endured.

As yet as a rookie Eli was only allowed to do a one night stop over, usually Stourbridge, one day there one day back again, this suited Jessie, she could go and stay at her mother's for one night at a time no problem – or so her story went - without One Arm Louis her official boyfriend being any the wiser.

They had it worked out to the last detail, Jessie would call in the chip shop, the one nearly out of town, Eli would pull into the bank and Jessie would jump aboard and hide down in the cabin until they were well out of town – you never knew who might see her and take great delight in telling One Arm Louis, who wouldn't take kindly to learn that his brand new girlfriend was having it away with his brand new boatman. Then when they were out in the country they would moor up and eat a tasty supper; Jessie usually providing the 'afters'. She didn't mind, in fact she looked upon it as her sacred duty to educate Eli the best she could, after all he had been married to Myrtle and as a consequence he needed all the education he could get.

Yes, Jessie had been disappointed in Eli for the first trip or two, but with her expertise – and her unfortunate mother continually having those relapses - it hadn't been long before Eli had improved tremendously, his only regret that he couldn't show off his new expertise on his missus, he would show her a thing or two and make her realise what she was missing.

But every time Eli thought that, he would turn over in the little bed in the cabin at the stern of his vessel, gaze upon the beautiful woman lying next to him and silently say 'bugger you Myrtle, and your creepy mother', he would then smile and thank whichever god happened to be on duty that night for a wonderful life.

Even his zits had disappeared.

One Arm was pleased with Eli's progress, he was a little disappointed that Jessie's mother kept falling ill, but he didn't say too much, in case Jessie got the hump, left him and in a fit of nostalgia went back to Chugger Riley and her gas lamp.

It is Enoch we should feel sorry for, he was stuck at home with his wife Mona – Mona by name and moaner by nature – except for the occasional visit to the pub and his allotment. Not for him the freedom of the open canal and Jessie's legs. All Mona seemed to do these days was moan about Eli,

"'E's never at 'ome, I was only saying to Mrs Digby the other day, whatever does our Eli do I said, no wonder Myrtle left 'im, 'e's never at 'ome, no good ever come of letting your old mon stay away from 'ome days on end." She took a breath, "'E's up to no good, I said to 'er, I said, you mark my words, Mrs Digby, you mark my words, yo see if I ay right!"

"Of course he's never at home, you dopey bat, he works on the canals now, doe 'e, 'e takes a boat full of whatever the cargo is from Tipton to Stourbridge or Birmingham wherever and that can take a week, the jammy beggar… He's damn lucky in my opinion."

Mona crossed her arms which doesn't have the same effect as when Jessie crosses her legs and pursed her lips.

"The best day's work Myrtle ever did was leave that idiot and go back to 'er mother!"

Enoch headed for the back door. "If leavin' 'ome's that bloody clever why doe thee do the same?"

The blue and white flower vase missed his head by inches. On his way to work Enoch was getting more and more depressed by the minute. It didn't seem fair – not that he begrudged his brother anything – that Eli was a happy bunny sampling the twin delights of the open road as it were and when her mother was ill Jessie's legs while he was still living with the harridan from hell.

Standing by his lathe in the machine shop where he spent what seemed like every daylight hour Enoch brooded, he only had three cups of tea and two bacon sandwiches in the tea break, the foreman was worried.

"Yo look like death warmed up, why doe thee go and see the nuss, our kid?"

Enoch shook his head, it wasn't a nurse he needed, it was freedom….he sighed deeply, he looked around the workshop, a life-long prison for a crime he had never committed, no parole until he reached sixty five, a vision of his missus standing with her arms crossed and a frown on her face that could peel sprouts entrenched in his mind… freedom from…all…yes, that was it, freedom from everything!

Of course, that was it…. Freedom, that was what Enoch needed, that and someone like Jessie to spend his nights with of course, that would help, but initially freedom, is that too much to ask? It's my life, so it should be my decision what I do with it.

By the end of the day as he clocked off he knew what to do.

Enoch's new life

"You want me to set you on a as a boatman?"

"Yes please, Mister Ferrari."

"Why?"

Why indeed…… "I don't want to work in a factory any more, I want a job where I can enjoy life a bit more."

One Arm Louis liked Enoch, he, like his brother Eli was an antidote to the sleazy stab-you-in-the-back chancers he usually had to deal with.

"Enjoy life… translated does that mean a job where you can skive off with nobody knowing?"

Enoch smiled, "No, sir, it is only necessary to skive when you are in a job you don't like."

The perfect answer.

One Arm Louis nodded. "Listen lad, I don't have a vacancy on a boat just at the moment…"

He saw Enoch's face change, he saw the disappointment. "But… as a stop-gap until one becomes available I can offer you the job as yard foreman, in charge of making sure the boats get loaded on time, that sort of thing. You wouldn't be spending much time actually afloat as it were but it's a start, and at least you would be making your own decisions – under guidance from me, of course."

One Arm Louis was inventing a job that previously had never existed, a yard foreman, he had always done the job himself, but in his eyes he owed Enoch as he owed Eli. Yes, he thought, it might work, he will follow my orders and if leave him to carry those orders out I will have a bit more time to myself and the welfare of my new secretary. Yes, thank you Enoch.

Enoch went home a happy man, even when his wife tackled him about why he was late he didn't rise to the bait.

He handed in his notice the following morning and without a backward glance walked out that same lunchtime, he simply couldn't be bothered to work his notice.

Arriving home he was just in time to meet the rent man coming out the back door. The rent man blushed, spluttered a 'good day, Enoch' and trotted off at some speed down the entry.

63

Enoch at this point suspected nothing, not until he went in to the front parlour to find his ever- obviously not so - faithful missus absolutely starkers on the sofa – apart from a paper hat on her head and a fairy wand in her hand

He should have been disappointed, he should have been shocked, maybe even distraught but in fact he felt relieved. She flustered and spluttered crying out that it wasn't how it seemed and why was he home so early.

"If it ay what it seems, what the 'ell is it?"

He pointed to the fairy wand, "granted 'im 'is wish did thee?" She tried to speak, he cut her off.

"Never mind, I doe care. Do you know what, I really doe care, 'e con 'ave thee, oh, sorry, actually I'm too late aren't I, it looks as if 'e already 'as."

He went upstairs, should I be feeling numb or something, he thought. It took only moments to pack his suitcase, he didn't have a lot to pack.

When he stepped off the bottom step of the stairs back into the parlour she was fully dressed.

"What dun thee want for thee tea?"

He couldn't believe it, here she was caught red handed as it were, and she wanted to know what he wanted for his tea!

"I doe want nothing, not tonight, not any night, I'm leaving." She burst into tears…. "Yo cor leave me, what'll I do without thee?"

He sniffed, "Yo've been doin' all right without me so far." He closed the door on his way out.

There would be a bed for him at Eli's place, Eli was halfway between here and Stourbridge.

No, the allotment would be better, it wasn't fair to break into Eli's, yes the allotment would do fine… It would have to do fine for a long time yet, he thought, at least until I work out what to do next.

It did occur to him that since breakfast he had got shot of the job he hated and detested and without any help from him his missus had got shot of him. The two things in his life that gave him the most grief…gone. Who would have believed it? Life was improving all the time.

Waving to a few of the allotment holders he opened the door to his new home. He wondered if a hammock might work, or more seriously how about a camp bed. Double of course, you never know your luck.

The sofa would be fine for now. He tidied the place up a bit and set off for the corner shop, food and the basic necessities of life would have to be the next job, and then once this desirable residence was organised and he had managed a night's sleep it was off to work in a brand new job in a brand new morning.

A brand new beginning in fact.

That thought he found to be quite exciting.

Enoch knew some of the men at the docks and they genuinely seemed pleased to see him. "Welcome to the gang, Enoch," bawled Nosher from the opposite bank, "Yo'r Eli wo 'alf gerra shock when 'e sees thee 'ere."

One Arm Louis came walking up from his office to meet Enoch, he smiled and shook Enoch's hand, "are you ready to learn a new job, Enoch?"

"Just as ready as I am to forget the last one, sir."

As One Arm took Enoch to show him the ropes he went through this first part of the day doing what he would have done anyway, he showed Enoch what he was doing telling him that in a day or two he would be on his own, "but don't guess, if unsure come and ask".

Enoch nodded, he had visions of doing a lot of asking.

"You are not going to get fed up with me asking, then?"

"No, I'd sooner you did that rather than we get the schedules all over the place…. Don't worry, it'll all become clear in a couple of days or so."

One Arm walked over to another shed, as he did so he explained what was going to happen.

"In this shed we keep what we call the perishables, food and the like. For instance today we have a large consignment of mushy peas in forty gallon barrels to ship to Bristol where they will put on board an ocean-going freighter to New York. Just like France, very big in America is mushy peas."

It has to be said that Mushy peas is pretty big in the Black Country as well, every innovative fish and chip shop proprietor from Sutton Coldfield down to Coventry got through at least one barrel of mushy peas a week; and so they should, after all mushy peas is the caviar of the Black Country and we are very proud of that.

One Arm explained that he was lucky to get this particular export contract to New York, Chugger Riley had been after it for years.

"It is our job, up to now it's been me, but pretty soon to it'll be thee, for instance for today to allocate a boat to take the barrels to Bristol, as it happens I have already done this, but you will do it yourself once you have got the hang of it.

Today we are sending 'President', skipper Cornelious Wood, he is a very experienced skipper, he comes from a long line of boatmen, about the fourth or fifth generation I believe."

They arrived at the door of the shed, One Arm noticed that the door was ajar, it shouldn't be....

There was what looked like a green stain on the gravel...

Worse, whatever it was it was actually pouring under the door, across the towpath and into the canal.

One Arm worked hard to get the door open more, he was working against the tide...a slow moving almost sinister green tide.

Inside was a green larval mess, the barrels had all been smashed open, every one of them, presumably during the night and the contents, something like two thousand gallons of mushy peas, and the last of it was still oozing out of the smashed barrels, had contrived to cover the whole floor of the shed. One Arm and Enoch struggled to keep their feet it was like walking on ice.

Just at that moment 'President' pulled up at the canal bank, its skipper tying up at the stern.

Cornelius the skipper had a shock when he jumped ashore and saw the mess.

Within seconds there was a tidy crowd gathered to see the disaster, on everyone's lips were the words 'Chugger Riley', it seemed obvious, Chugger was getting his own back for the secret groaty pudding recipe disaster.

But would he be this obvious, thought One Arm?

One Arm Louis and Enoch stood entranced as they watched the green ooze spill over the towpath and sploosh into the canal, and as they stood open-mouthed it turned its water green.

Enoch had heard the men whisper 'Chugger Riley'.

"What do you think?" asked Enoch, 'is it Chugger, dun thee reckon?"

One Arm Louis didn't know, but he intended to find out, meanwhile someone had to contact the mushy peas factory, he needed another two thousand gallons, barrelled up, and quick, they had to get to Bristol to catch the freighter to Marseilles.

One Arm shook his head, this was going to cost him a tidy packet, whoever it was was going to pay, and he didn't necessarily mean with money.

One Arm instructed his men to check all the other sheds for damage, it looked like someone had been on a wrecking spree.

He was surprised to learn that nothing else had been touched, no damage whatsoever anywhere else in the yard, only the mushy peas.

What the heck was going on?

A council of war was called in the snug of The Fountain Inn, effective immediately and as the new docks foreman Enoch was invited to attend.

He was shocked to realise that he was sitting amongst One Arm's chosen few, the gang, the men who didn't scar their hands working on the dock, they were kept for the hard work of keeping One Arm's business top of the pile.

Enoch was introduced, they didn't seem to care who he was, actually they were suspicious, not of Enoch per se but of any one they regarded as an outsider to their select group. They knew and trusted each other, if necessary with their lives but an outsider couldn't be trusted until he had proved himself.

One Arm intended that Enoch should prove himself.

It was agreed by the gang that no action should be taken against Chugger Riley until they had proof, after all, it could be someone else, not likely perhaps but always possible.

One Arm had no intention of putting his head above the parapet and attracting the attention of the police, certainly not reporting this act of extreme vandalism, canal people had their own way of enforcing the law – their own law; all they had to do was prove, and not necessarily beyond any shadow of a doubt that it was Chugger Riley and then they would act – and it wouldn't be pretty.

The plan was this, various members of the gang were to scour the pubs and caffs of the town trying to pick up any bits of gossip, the others had to gain entry to the other boat yards ostensibly to find out if they had also been targeted by whoever it was had taken a dislike to mushy peas, but this was purely a ruse to sniff around for anything vaguely suspicious.

"Remember boys, we ay got proof it was Chugger even though we think it was, so check on everybody just I case it ay 'im.."

Enoch was to be allocated a special job…

He would accompany Cornelius Wood on President to Bristol when the new consignment had been delivered from the mushy peas factory and loaded up.

He was to expect trouble…………….

One consignment had been destroyed, would the next be any safer?

Thanks a bunch, thought Enoch.

Maybe a factory bench was a pretty good bet after all.

No, he had made his choice, he would stick it out.

The mushy peas factory worked through the rest of the day and through the night to get a new consignment ready. A convoy of carts pulled by Shire horses carried the barrels to the docks where a specially selected gang of men were waiting to load up.

It was almost twelve o'clock mid-day by the time President was loaded, they were twenty four hours behind schedule and they had to hope that Cornelius would make good time.

"Travel all night, Corny, instruct Enoch during the daytime, he will do his share, he's a bright enough lad, he should pick it up quite easily…You know what is at stake my friend."

One Arm started to walk away but had a thought.

"Tell you what, take Colin with you, (Colin was a horse used for pulling canal boats that didn't have an engine). We can't expect the motor to work twenty four hours a day for several days, give it a rest to cool down when you can and use Colin where there's a decent towpath. "

Cornelius agreed with that. But….

"If I might ask, One Arm, why can't I take one of the lads who already know how to steer a boat and work the locks, to say nothing of how to handle Colin?"

"Because…. Enoch has only just started with us today, so whoever it was did this damage it can't be him, he wouldn't even know about the mushy peas barrels, but we don't know for sure if it wasn't one or more of the other lads, not for sure, and I want someone with you that both you – and I – can trust."

Cornelius nodded his head, he appreciated being trusted, not only that his boss made sense.

"You are right boss, Enoch will learn all about steering a barge, working the locks and handling Colin by teatime."
Actually Colin was a very experienced horse and didn't need anyone to tell him what to do.
They shook hands, two old friends who knew that apart from themselves and the new boy they couldn't really trust anyone else – not for sure.
"Do your best, Corny, make up whatever time you can, and let's hope the freighter in Bristol Docks is still there when you arrive."
Cornelius would do his very best, especially as the boss had told him there would be a substantial bonus if he got there in time.
Colin was fitted with his harness, it was no bother he had done this more times than any other horse in the yard, he stood patiently waiting to head off along the towpath, which, although we will never know for sure, Colin seemed to prefer to hanging around in the stables or the yard.
Cornelius instructed Enoch what to do, it wasn't hard, Colin's harness was much easier to fit than normal tack.
Colin didn't seem to mind a total stranger, Enoch decided he liked horses.
Cornelius added the finishing touch, a silver plated fitting on the top of the harness from which a set of three bells were already tinkling every time Colin moved.
"Nice," smiled Enoch. "The finishing touch, looks lovely."
Corny nodded, "Ah lad, but that ain't all it do."
Enoch waited for an explanation.
"You see, lad, when the 'orse is walkin' along the towpath the bells give off a cheery tinklin' sound, this keeps the devil away and stops 'im from spookin' the 'orse and causing mishchief, 'cos the devil, 'e doe like cheery things, but he does like causing mischief thee knowst."
They were ready.

With no pomp and circumstance whatsoever Corny pulled away from the dock, next stop Bristol, he couldn't remember the last time he had been this nervous; Enoch led Colin alongside, Enoch wasn't nervous, he was scared stiff.

The plot and the mushy peas thickens

It wasn't long before some of the boys returned to the yard, all with the same story, another three yards at least had been broken in to overnight and the mushy peas destroyed, but the funny thing was, there was no other damage, just the mushy peas.

Knocker Jenkins Junior the son of Jenkins and Jenkins and Son, one of the largest carriers in the docks reckoned he'd lost over two hundred barrels, Jammy Dodger reckoned at least seventy, and so it went on, all the yards known to carry mushy peas had received a visit from whoever it was had an aversion to this exquisite delicacy.

One Arm quickly realised that whoever it was had the resources, it would have been impossible for just one gang to do the rounds all in one night, there must have been several separate gangs each knowing exactly where to go, so that meant they were organised, someone had been in charge, this wasn't vandalism, this was an act of war.

All this of course was unknown to Cornelius and Enoch, perhaps as well, Enoch was already having several breakdowns, every movement in the hedgerows meant there was some gangster poised ready to pounce – at least that was how his mind was working. He took some comfort from Colin, who was ambling along without a care in the world, there was nothing in the hedgerows that were spooking the horse so it must be okay. And every time Enoch told himself that he still didn't believe it.

"Are we likely to meet up with our Eli, Corny?" he called across to the skipper.

"Dunno, lad, it depends where his trip is."

"Stourbridge, I think."

"When did he leave the yard?"

"Early yesterday."

"Then yes, we might just meet him, it's only a two day round trip to Stourbridge, we should meet him on his way home." Enoch smiled, if they did, Eli would have a surprise to see his brother leading a horse along the towpath, and he would be able to have a good gawp at Jessie's legs – assuming she is with him.

One Arm Louis decided to take this 'war' a step further. His boys had visited most of the yards but not Chugger Riley's, this yard was notoriously hard to gain access to.

One Arm thought it might be a good idea to pay a surprise visit to Chugger Riley, one-time believer he could be the next MP for Tipton – until the groaty pudding blew up in his face as you might say.

Waiting for Boxer-Joe to arrive – Boxer had nothing to do with the canal boats, his job, now that he had retired from the bare knuckle fighting, was getting the orders, indeed when prospective clients saw Boxer-Joe approach they were usually only too happy to give him all the business he asked for – One Arm sat and thought this through, unfortunately even when Boxer arrived he was no nearer to a conclusion, it didn't make sense, who would break in to a yard – in fact several yards - just to sabotage one product?

One Arm, together with his trusty lieutenant walked down the towpath over the crossing bridge and straight through the front door of 'The Continental'.

One Arm knew which floor Chugger's private apartment was on so that was where he headed.

He knocked the door, if only for courtesies sake because the next second Boxer put his shoulder to the door and burst it open.

One Arm wondered if that wasn't a tad unnecessary but it was too late now, anyway Chugger would be knocked off-balance so it was impressive.

The sound of crunching wood brought Chugger running from the bedroom, closely followed by a girl who could best be described as not dressed. She screamed, threw her arms over the bits she felt like keeping secret and rushed back into the bedroom completely forgetting to cover her backside. Boxer-Joe clicked his approval.

"Very nice, Chugger, very nice indeed."

One Arm Louis smiled. "How does she compare with Jessie?" Chugger ignored both men, he headed straight for the door to inspect the damage.

"You will get the bill for this, One Arm, I don't understand why you employ thugs like him."

Boxer took exception to this but One Arm held him back, now wasn't the time.

"I'll do a deal with you, Chugger. I'll pay for the repair to the door but you pay for the destroyed barrels of mushy peas....
And if there is no more damage to my mushy peas Boxer will do no more damage to your door, but if there is any more damage to my mushy peas I will not be answerable to the damage he might do to thee."

Chugger regained his composure with admirable calm.
He faced off One Arm Louis.

"What mushy peas.... What do you mean *your* mushy peas?"
One Arm was still convinced Chugger was responsible.

"*My* mushy peas, and mushy peas from several other yards...all destroyed."

Chugger frowned, he rang a little silver bell on the table, almost immediately a Chinese servant scuttled into the room.
"Tea, Chan."

Still giving an outward appearance of total calm,
Indian or Chinese, gentlemen?"
"Indian," replied One Arm Louis. "lemon, no sugar".
"Brown," replied Boxer-Joe. "condensed milk, no lemon."
Three cups, Chan," ordered Chugger, ignoring Boxer-Joe's
inexcusable ignorance of the English national drink.
The servant bowed and disappeared.
"Please sit, One Arm, you too Boxer."
Chugger remained standing. "One Arm, we have never been
friends, I would like to say we have never been enemies –
aside for that groaty pudding fiasco, which I am prepared to
concede started out as a bit of honest rivalry, which we do all
the time, all of us in this business not just between you and
me – but it maybe went into the realms of fantasy and totally
out of our - your – control, but we have never actually
despised each other sufficient to destroy a consignment of
mushy... mushy...." Chugger had a nasty thought. "Oh, my
God...."
"Come with me."
The Chinese servant brought the tea on a silver tray.
"Pour it Chan, we won't be long.. Come on, you two."
Chugger rushed out of the apartment and down the stairs
followed by One Arm Louis and Boxer-Joe.
Almost running across the yard he called for two of his men to
join him. Quite breathless he stopped outside the doors of a
large shed.
"Get these doors open, and quickly," he snapped. The two
men grappled with the long baulk of wood that went from side
to side of the doors."
"Hurry up!"
"We need the key to the lock, boss...." One asked rather
timidly.
"No we doe," answered the other man. "It ay locked."
Chugger started panicking, "of course it's bloody locked....
Oh my God, it ay locked. I locked it myself yesterday after we

had received that consignment of mushy peas for France....
Get the doors open, come on, we ay got all day!"
The doors were swung open to reveal a green swamp, there
were smashed barrels as far as the eye could see into the dark
and gloomy shed, the contents were oozing all over the floor,
and now that the doors were open allowing free passage the
green ooze flowed inexorably across the towpath and blooped
into the canal enhancing the colour which was already a
lovely pea green colour, courtesy of the escaped mushy peas
from One Arm's shed.
Chugger slid down the side of the shed and ended on the floor
with his knees under his chin and his head in his hands.
One Arm had a certain amount of sympathy, after all the
groaty pudding episode was pretty much his invention, and as
Chugger had said it had sort of taken over and make itself into
a monster under no-one's control.
"It looks as if Boxer-Joe ay gotta break your legs after all,
Chugger."
Chugger looked up at One Arm Louis.
"Thanks a bunch, now help me up... I don't suppose you
realise how serious this is?"
He motioned for his two men to get lost.
"Of course I do," snapped One Arm. "Of course I realise how
serious this is, everybody seems to have been targeted by
whoever did this."
Chugger shook his head. "I don't give a toss for the others.
Listen One Arm, keep this to yourself, but this consignment
of mushy peas was to be my last chance. Since the groaty
pudding embarrassment I have lost a lot of business, they
won't deal with me, they are calling me a piss-artist, conning
them all out of forty quid each. The fact that it all went to
charity they don't give a toss about..... I have been accused of
taking money from those who can best afford it, and they
don't like it."
One Arm smiled, he had heard that, he remembered laughing.

Chugger continued, "The destination for these mushy peas is Paris, that's in France, where they haven't heard of the groaty pudding nonsense… I have no other business and now this has happened I don't have a business at all."

This was news to One Arm, he almost felt guilty.

He sighed, the solution to this problem wasn't simply to hang Chugger upside down from a gantry over the canal until he confessed or they would drop him in it, because it obviously wasn't him.

One Arm was thinking, and thinking fast.

"I am going to call a meeting of the yard owners, seven o'clock tonight in The Fountain Inn. Okay with you?"

Chugger nodded, whatever, it was okay with him.

Meanwhile back on the canal

Meanwhile, oblivious to the gaining pace of the catastrophe back at the yards, Enoch, Cornelius and Colin were making good time, there had been no hold-ups, the locks had all been in their favour, the motor was 'chugging' along nicely – now you know where Chugger got his nickname – and everything in the garden, or at least along the towpath was rosy.

Enoch was getting used to the rustlings in the hedgerows, occasionally he would spot a field mouse, a hedgehog or maybe a bank vole, he had never realised just how busy a long line of bushes and a ditch could be.

Instructed by Cornelius he allowed Colin to browse the shrubs along the way when the horse spied something tasty, it stopped Colin from getting bored and supplemented the nose bag making the feed go further.

Cornelius wondered if he should instruct Enoch on the finer points of browsing for human consumption, after all it is possible to almost live from what may be found along the towpath, as many boat families did, but figured that Enoch had enough to think about just for now.

Order! Order!

The boatyard owners, shippers and canal boat operators were gathered in the function room of The Fountain Inn Tipton.

Order.... Order.... One Arm was having trouble controlling the meeting.

Order....Order...

'Mine's a pint,' shouted someone.

"One at a time, please, and you cheapskates can buy your own....Gentlemen, we are not going to get anywhere if we all shout at once... If I can't get order I shall ask Boxer-Joe to do so and he has his own methods."

The room went quiet, which should be no surprise.

"The meeting is all yours, Brother One Arm," this was Jagger Stone.

"Thank you, Brother Jagger, the minutes will so show."

One Arm gathered his thoughts.

"Gentlemen, we are faced with a potential catastrophe..."

Murmurings of agreement rippled around the room.

"Someone somewhere is determined to put us out of business vis a vis the mushy peas trade, but first of all we have to elect a chairman for this meeting, and if my fears prove to be correct possibly many more meetings to come until we have this situation back under our control."

Chugger banged his pint pot on the table. "I propose Brother One Arm Louis Ferrari for Chairman."

This came as a surprise to many in the room, it was well known that Chugger and One Arm disliked each other, especially after the groaty pudding fiasco..

Chugger read the room. "I propose One Arm because he has the resources, and the organisational skills, and just in case anyone was wondering, this situation is so serious, especially to some of us it will be advantageous to keep personal feelings out of it.

One Arm nodded his agreement. "Thank you Brother Chugger… If there are no other proposals…."

Brother Jagger stuck his hand up. "I propose that we have joint chairmen, Brother One Arm and Brother Chugger, that way if we have to call an extraordinary meeting and one of them is unavailable we will still have an already pre-elected chairman."

"I'll second that," this was Brother Knocker.

Brilliant, everyone thought this was a great idea and the proposal was passed unanimously.

"Okay…" One Arm nodded.

"If it is okay with you Brother Chugger, this meeting will be conducted under my jurisprudence, unless you…?"

Chugger acknowledged the suggestion and shook his head. "I'm good, you are today's Chair, Brother One Arm, let the minutes so show."

Fine, except there was no-one taking the minutes.

Apart from Dum-dum McAdams – and he could neither read nor write, so not a lot of help - no-one volunteered so they shrugged off this un-necessary formality and carried on.

It was noted with some surprise by many in the room that this must be the first time in living memory that One Arm Louis Ferrari and Chugger Riley had agreed on anything which only goes to show just how serious this situation is.

Chugger banged his pint pot on the table again, "Under your jurisprudence then, Brother One Arm."

Neither One Arm nor Chugger had a clue what 'jurisprudence' meant but it sounded good, and the room was impressed.

"Brothers…." Announced One Arm, "it is estimated that between us we have lost over five hundred barrels of mushy peas… The extraordinary fact is there has been no damage to any other product we have had stored in our sheds. This can only mean that the perpetrator of this vile crime has a vested interest in the destruction of all mushy peas in captivity or he has a psychological problem and has a thing against or even for mushy peas."

"Sex" muttered Jobie Wood, "it all comes down to sex, at the end of the day it all comes down to sex.

"Unless it clashes with me darts night," shouted someone."

That got a laugh.

All eyes were on Brother Jobie. He was known as something of an intellectual, when he was a nipper he once went to school for a whole week, every single day.

Chugger and One Arm swapped glances, Chugger raised his hand, One Arm motioned for him to speak.

"The Chair acknowledges Brother Chugger."

Brother Chugger coughed to clear his throat.

"Brother Jobie," muttered Chugger gently, "most of the boys here are happily married – up to a point – I doubt there is any one of us, except for your good-self obviously, who has ever had the urge to have sex with a barrel of mushy peas," he smiled indulgently at Brother Jobie, "rolling round in the green ooze gets you going, does it?"

The assembled had a good laugh at Brother Jobie's expense, the mood lightened and One Arm was able to continue.

"Item one, who is the perpetrator, and what are we going to do about it? Let the records so show – that is if we were keeping records - that there is no item two."

Allowing a few minutes for the boys to get another pint from the bar, One Arm Louis and Chugger Riley put their heads together, this was a crisis and the only outcome had to be success, which meant their own personal co-operation was important or they were all in the clart.

The boys sat down... One Arm gave them a minute to settle.

"Knocker, put the crib board away, we are not here to play cards."

Judging the moment was right Brother One Arm banged his glass on the table, immediately the room went quiet.
"Item One….." One Arm started the meeting proper.

Surprise, surprise

They still had a long way to go, Bristol was a fair old distance at the best of times but it seemed further when it was in the back of your mind that you might be hijacked at any moment and all your barrels of mushy peas rolled into the cut.
Cornelius throttled back, he had seen something in the distance.
He called to Enoch and pointed.
Enoch screwed up his eyes.
"It's a canal boat."
Corny snorted, "I can see that, but why is it kind of sideways on blocking the cut?"
Good question.
"It's like as if someone has deliberately blocked the cut and don't want us to go any furth…… whoops!"
Corny nodded, he had already come to that conclusion.
He pulled President into the bank, jumped off, tied the vessel to an overhanging branch and concentrated his eyes down the canal. Yes, there was a canal boat pretty much sideways on and definitely blocking their passage but he could see no-one, if this was an ambush whoever it was must be hiding behind the hedges.
"What do think, Corny?" Enoch was shivering, and it wasn't that cold, not for the time of year.
"I think we are in trouble, that's what I think."
"Can't we turn round and go back?"
Corny shot a withering glance at his companion. "This boat is three times as long as the cut is wide, just how are we going to turn round? And it's a hell of a long way back to Tipton going backwards!"

"Sssh!" Enoch put his finger to his lips. "I think I hear summat!"

He pointed to the hedge bottom. "It's coming out of there!"

"There must be a million creepy crawly things scuttling around an 'edge bottom, of course you can hear summat!"

Corny was having his doubts about the usefulness of his crew. But Enoch was undaunted.

"How many creepy crawlies in your experience shout 'help', admittedly very quietly…. There is someone down in that ditch shouting help… We are going to have to check this out, I wonder who it can be…." Then he had a thought. "Maybe it is someone trying to lure us down into the 'edge bottom so that they can cosh us and nick our boat!"

Corny was having other ideas, he suddenly realised he recognised the boat that was still cutting off their passage. It was 'Ruby', Eli's boat.

He turned to Enoch. "It isn't anyone waiting to cosh us, I think you might find it is yo'r Eli down in that 'edge bottom, almost certainly trussed up like a chicken and gagged which is why he is shouting his 'ead off very quietly!"

Enoch scrambled down the bank and almost disappeared into the ditch, it was pretty steep and very wet.

Suddenly he stopped, he couldn't believe it….

His eyes were glued to a pair of legs, a pair of female legs he recognised, they belonged to Jessie. What was Jessie doing down in a hedge bottom….?

"Stupid question, Enoch.." sneered Corny, "in the absence of a gas lamp an 'edge bottom will do very nicely."

"Doe be daft, Corny, 'er's all fastened up with ropes and stuff… 'Er cor be up to nothing trussed up like 'er is, no matter 'ow kinky 'er might be."

"I ay kinky, thank you very much", snapped Jessie as Enoch untied the gag around her mouth.

Enoch wondered why he hadn't thought of a gag years ago for his missus.

He unfastened Jessie's legs making sure he took full advantage of the situation. Finally he untied her hands at which point she slapped him in the face.

"That's for grabbing my legs when yo should 'ave been grabbin' the rope…"

He only grinned. Next he untied his brother and the three of them scrambled up the bank and out of the hedge bottom.

"I'll bet that ay the fust time yo've been in an 'edge bottom, Jess!" laughed Corny.

"Shut your gob, Corny, yo'm only jealous. Do summat useful like go and put the kettle on" She replied.

They climbed aboard President, Eli and Jessie started to recover their composure a little then Jessie, after refusing the very generous offer from Enoch to do it for her she massaged her moving parts.

"I know it's the obvious question, Eli," Corny spoke as he poured the tea into tin mugs, "but 'ow come yo and 'er was in an 'edge bottom, it's obvious it wor for fun, not tied up like that?"

"Cos we was tied up and slung in by them what attacked us, we've been down there ages," answered Jessie, not waiting for her 'skipper' to answer.

Enoch went cold again, he didn't like the word 'attack'.

"They suddenly appeared out of the 'edge, jumped aboard, there wor nothin' we could do, we was outnumbered," moaned Eli, he had found a bruise on his forehead and was massaging it. Jessie kissed it better. It was a miracle.

"Outnumbered?" Corny frowned. They were a long way from their destination and somewhere out there were… how many?

"About seven, I think, answered Jessie, "certainly more than we could handle even with me swinging the lock key around my head."

"We'd better rescue 'Ruby' and see what they did to her," Corny was more concerned about the boat than her crew.

The thing was, when they climbed aboard Ruby they discovered there was no damage, neither was there anything nicked, it was as if there had been no-one aboard.

Corny didn't understand, whoever it was ambushed the crew, tied them up and slung them in a hedge bottom then did nothing to the boat?

"Did you hear what they said, Eli... Did they say anything at all, any clues as to what they were doing, it doe seem natural to do nothing to the barge after tying up yo two and dumping thee in a ditch."

Once again it was Jessie who answered. "They never shut up, gabbing away ten to the dozen they were."

Corny smiled, they were getting somewhere.

"Yes, my girl, but what did they say?"

Jessie was wiping mud off her legs which did nothing for Enoch.

"I've no idea."

"What? What dun thee mean, yo 'eard 'em gabbin' away but yo doe no know what they was saying?"

Eli shook his head, "of course we doe know what they was saying, they was spakin' in foreign!"

Enoch and Corny exchanged looks, what the hell was Eli talking about?

Enoch took over. "Foreign, our Eli, they was talkin' foreign? What dun thee mean, foreign, was they talkin' Brummy or summat?"

Eli shook his head, "'no, it wor Brummy, I doe think they was from Birmingham."

Jessie also shook her head, "No, Corny, it was proper foreign, It wouldn't surprise me if they wor even English!"

Corny was thinking... He still couldn't understand why Ruby had been left intact.... Wait a minute...

"Eli, ast thee got any mushy peas aboard?"

"What?"

"Ast got any barrels of mushy peas on Ruby?"

Eli shook his head, they hadn't heard of the mushy peas disaster back in the docks of course, he and Jessie had made a late start yesterday dinner time, it was supposed to have taken them the rest of the day to get to Stourbridge, unload overnight and then gently cruise back home the next day.
It was yesterday teatime when they were attacked, they hadn't even reached Stourbridge yet.
"I thought not, yo've got some pretty tasty cargo an' all, posh crockery come down from Stoke on Trent and stuff, but no mushy peas ...." mused Corny.
Enoch caught up. "They was only looking for mushy peas, wor they, Corny, they wor looking for anything else?"
Corny nodded his head, in as few sentences as possible he explained to Eli and Jessie what had happened back at base. They were open-mouthed with astonishment.
"If this lot was looking for mushy peas, they day find none 'cos we ay got none...." whispered Jessie, "and you know what that means?"
Once again Corny nodded. "It means they are still on the prowl for any boat what has.."
"And that means us," whispered Enoch.
Just for once Enoch's brain found something else to think about besides Jessie's legs.

Back at The Fountain Inn they were getting no-where, it was obvious to Brother One arm Louis Ferrari and Brother Chugger Riley that from the sea of anxious faces before them the perpetrators were outsiders and not canal men, every man in the room was extremely worried indeed, as someone had already suggested, it's mushy peas today, what will it be tomorrow?
Apart from setting up security patrols made up of men from all the different yards so as to combat any suspicion of each other there seemed little else they could do, they would simply have to be extremely vigilant.

Jammy Dodger was looking vacant.

"Vigilant means keep your eyes open, Jammy…" explained Chugger.

Suddenly they were interrupted when Tony the Pizza burst into the room, he was extremely out of breath, he collapsed into a chair.

"Thank heaven you are here, One Arm…. I've run all the way."

"What's up, Tony?" shouted Chugger, although he knew for sure it could only be more bad news, any animosity he had towards Tony the Pizza meant nothing right at this moment. Tony the Pizza took a slurp from a pint pot handed to him….

"It's the mushy peas factory, Chugger, *The mushy peas factory is on fire!*"

Be On Your Guard

"What are we going to," asked Jessie, "Do we carry on?"

Corny nodded, "We have to, we have a job to do."

"Tell you what," mused Eli. "I'm only going as far as Stourbridge and up to now I haven't got far, you are going to Bristol, what we'll do is this, we go in convoy, I'll leave Ruby and Jessie in Stourbridge –I am sure Jess will find something to amuse her - and then I'll come with you to Bristol; maybe, just maybe, whoever this is won't attack if they see a boat with a crew of three."

"Four," corrected Jessie. "I'm coming with you."

She felt she ought to be annoyed at Eli's reference to her finding something to amuse her, she wasn't like that anymore, but now wasn't the time, she would get her own back when one night he felt a bit amorous and she could push him out of the bunk.

"Won't One Arm Louis worry if you don't get back to the yard on time, Eli?" Enoch just wondered.

"Of course he will, our kid, but I think he would sooner worry about me and Ruby being late than worry about yet another expensive consignment of mushy peas floating off down the canal."

That made sense.

"That means," added Corny, "If we do as One Arm said and carry on travelling day and night we can have a crew of two on duty at all times, sounds good to me.

"I'm no boatman, so you will probably say I know nothing;" Jessie was frowning, she was still smarting from Eli's crass remark, "but what about we travel down the middle of the canal, that way any-one wanting to attack us will have to jump halfway across the cut and all we will have to worry about are the bridges when some brave soul could jump off one and on to President.."

Contrary to saying that Jessie knew nothing they all agreed it sounded like a good policy, they quickly agreed, and prompted by Corny, Eli apologised to Jessie.

The rest of the day went without a hitch, they took it in turns to crew the vessel and look after Colin and by sunset they had done well.

Corny objected to the suggestion from Eli - who simply wanted to spend a little time with Jessie alone but wouldn't dare say so - that they moored up for the night, partly because that would make them vulnerable to attack and partly because One Arm Louis had insisted that they travel through the night, but mostly because Corny kept thinking about the substantial bonus One Arm had promised him should he succeed in getting to Bristol before the freighter left.

Back at The Fountain Inn the place was in uproar, questions were being fired at Tony the Pizza who was fielding them the best he could.

Yes, the police were there.

Yes, there were loads of firemen.

Yes, the sheds containing the barrels of processed mushy peas were all destroyed in the conflagration.

"He means 'fire', Jammy," explained One Arm.

No, there was no hope for the building, it was well alight and had almost certainly been completely destroyed by now.

Several of the assembled wondered what fried mushy peas would taste like but they didn't dare ask, it would make them look as if they were treating the situation in a carefree and flippant manner, maybe even point the finger of suspicion.

"At least the fuzz can't accuse us," mused Chugger, after Boxer-Joe had gained control of the rabble.

"What dun thee mean, Chugger," asked Knocker.

"I mean that we, that is everyone who works in the yards have been here for at least an hour, so it cor be one of us."

One Arm raised his hand. "That has never stopped the fuzz from trying to pin stuff on us before, but on this occasion as a last resort – and I know we said we wouldn't involve the cops, but like I say as a last resort - if they do come sniffing around chucking accusations like confetti we will have to show them the mess in the sheds, even the cops won't believe we are hell bent on wrecking our own businesses."

The meeting broke up, there seemed little else they could do, only be as careful as possible and report back anything that looked in the least suspicious.

As they dispersed, some to go back to work, some to go home, some to their wives, some to their girlfriends, some who couldn't decide which, but all via the public bar One Arm pulled Chugger to one side.

"Have you got a couple of bicycles, Brother Chugger?"

Chugger stared at One Arm, what was he talking about?

"Yes, I have as it happens, why?"

"So have I…Meet me by my yard in fifteen minutes complete with two bicycles, a willing volunteer and a flask of tea, I will be there with my own bikes and Boxer-Joe."

"Why?"

"Because the only mushy peas left in existence – and until the mushy peas factory has been re-built there won't be any more - are those on President which as we speak is somewhere between here and oblivion if this mob gets to it before we do. Listen… Come with me to find Corny and the consignment of mushy peas and I'll give you twenty five per cent of the profits….. But only if we get to see them safely aboard the freighter."

"Fifty fifty."

One Arm shook his head, "Sixty forty in my favour."

"Why your favour?"

One Arm smiled, "They are my mushy peas."

"They shook hands. "Done."

Chugger knew that One Arm was handing him a life-line, he had only haggled because it was force of habit, was this a kind of apology from One Arm for the groaty pudding nonsense? Probably, but who cares, it might save Chugger's bacon. They had shaken hands, that was a binding contract and Chugger knew that whatever he thought of One Arm Louis Ferrari, his new partner would never renege on a hand shake, sacrosanct is a handshake so they both hurried off to find their bicycles and trusty travelling companions.

"Better still," called One Arm as an afterthought, "Ask for volunteers, any-one with a bike who fancies a punch-up. Tell 'em come with us and there's a quid for every man."

Chugger grinned, that sounded more like it, a proper army. It would be dark in a couple of hours but there was so much at stake they couldn't let that bother them, besides they couldn't get lost all they had to do was follow the towpath and as it would be a full moon which would reflect off the still water showing them the way they wouldn't even need a torch.

Within the hour One Arm Louis, Boxer-Joe, Chugger Riley, Jammy Dodger and twenty three willing lads, each with a pound note tucked safely in their back pockets were peddling like stink down the towpath and heading south.

Pirates

Ruby was wedged fast between the banks but with a few deft pushes controlled by Corny, President soon unhooked Ruby's nose from the undergrowth on the opposite bank and before long she was alongside the towpath.
After checking for damage Corny declared Ruby fit for work so off they went, next stop Stourbridge – they hoped.
Corny and Enoch on President, Eli and Jessie on Ruby, while Colin, who knew exactly what to do, walked alongside. On the odd occasion he found something tasty in the hedgerow he took his time, gobbled it up, savoured whatever it was and then trotted back to the convoy.

"Jessie," called Corny, "yo said yo'd been down that 'edge bottom for ages, it might 'ave felt like ages, but Ruby wor 'olding up any traffic so it couldn't 'ave been very long or there would 'ave been a load of barges trying to get through."
"I wondered that," nodded Enoch.
I'll bet you didn't, thought Corny.
"So to me, that means only one thing…." continued Corny.
Eli interrupted. "It means that whoever it was ay very far away, and they'll be looking for barges carrying mushy peas, just like we've got, isn't that nice!"
It was a sobering thought.

They were still a good few miles from Stourbridge but the signs were good, they had experienced no scares, no strange happenings and maybe, just maybe they might get away with it. If they could reach Stourbridge they stood a chance, they would then have a crew of four on one vessel, surely this would deter even the most ardent pirate.
"I'm sorry, Jess, I only meant it as a joke. I know that particular way of life is behind you, and I don't condemn you for it, it must have been hard for you. I wish you well in this

new life, and I am proud to be a part of it, it just narks me a tad to know that I have to play second fiddle to One Arm Louis.. Okay, I know I can't give you what he gives you, jewels and stuff but that doesn't stop me from thinking a lot of you, and I do, you know."

"Do what, Eli?"

"Think a lot of you."

"Do you mean that, Eli?"

"Of course I do… Let me tell you summat, I think a lot more of you than I did Myrtle, even on our wedding day."

That took her breath away.

"Are you serious?"

"I've never been more serious."

No man had ever told Jessie he had feelings for her, only what he wanted from her.

"Then, I have to ask, if you didn't… I mean…. If you…didn't love her, then why did you marry her?"

Eli shrugged, "She told me she was pregnant… Worse, she told her mother and father she was pregnant, and her father made it plain I didn't have a choice, it was a shotgun wedding, at least it would have been a shotgun wedding if he could have borrowed one. So marry her I did, for better or for worse…."

Jessie gave him a little cuddle. "And you are still waiting for the better," she whispered.

"Not any more, Jess… The better arrived quite unexpectedly and only recently."

He kissed her, "and it is standing right next to me, I have never been so happy."

She felt like crying. After what she had done to earn a crust how can any man say he had feelings for her….?

Don't knock it, Jess, she thought, just do your best to hang on to him, 'cos it 'll be a long time before you find another one like him.

"And was she, your wife, I mean?"

"Was she what, Jess?"

"Preggers."

"Nope."

Unexpectedly he started laughing. "My God, I was the innocent, it never occurred to me until after we was wed that she couldn't be pregnant 'cos she had never let me…. er… you know, before we was married but I still bloody fell for it."

"You are kidding me."

"Nope, later she told me that she only married me 'cos she was fed up of going to chapel every Sunday and she knew I didn't go at all so therefore I wouldn't make her go like her father did; and she said she'd got pregnant through lusting after Rudolph Valentino so much it put her in the club."

"And I suppose you fell for that as well," Jessie couldn't help but smile.

"Yep, she told me she had written to him explaining the situation but all he sent her was a signed photograph. Then in the absence of anyone bearing a passing likeness to Rudolph Valentino she chose me, but the disappointment of our honeymoon not only dampened her ardour but caused an almighty fart which put an end to her phantom pregnancy." Jessie looked at Eli and shook her head, there was nothing else to do or say.

Keeping close order behind Ruby Corny stuck like glue. He figured that if someone did manage to get aboard it would be but a short jump for one crew from one boat to the other to help out. He knew Jessie could look after herself, he had seen her in action with the randy drunks on a Saturday night who were trying to cop a feel, what he didn't know was whether Enoch and Eli would be any good in a scrap.

Little did he know he was soon to find out.

"Eli!" called Corny, he thought he had seen something.

"I think I saw someone on that next bridge"

Eli screwed up his eyes against the setting sun, he could see nothing… wait, yes he could, a head, bobbing up and down above the parapet… Then he saw another, and another… there was a whole army of heads….

It was too late to stop the boat, it takes ages to stop a canal boat, it's not the same as a horse and cart and before Eli knew it he was under the bridge. Suddenly several ropes were slung over the parapet which dropped down to almost reach the deck of the boat…. It rained bodies, men shinned down the ropes and landed agilely on Ruby. Then running along the scuppers to the stern, pushing Eli and Jessie roughly aside, with a leap every one of them jumped across onto the prow of President, where they stopped and planned their next move. They crept silently towards the stern of President where Corny and Enoch were frozen in fear, two against seven wasn't the best deal you could think of….

"Take the tiller, Jess, our kid needs help." With his head down Eli made his way to the prow ready to take his life in his hands, he jumped across to President ready to play his part and take on the pirates, who so far hadn't noticed him.

Ignoring Eli Jessie followed her admirer, how could she not, he was the only man in her life who had expressed feelings for her, not a good enough excuse to get your head bashed in but what the hell she was going to stand by him even if…. Even if…. She didn't want to think about it.

With great presence of mind she had remembered to pick up the lock key.

"What the hell, Jess, I thought I told you …"

She placed her finger on his lips. "Shut up, I read a book once, something about all for one and one for something… Okay, let's do it."

They bounded forward, both shouting their heads off which was enough to scare anyone while Jessie waved the lock key around her head and Eli brandishing a boat hook that had been lying in the scuppers of President.

With the element of surprise two of the invaders were despatched almost immediately, one over the side and the other with a nasty gash to his head roughly the shape of a lock key, that narrowed the odds a little.

Enoch called to his brother, "well done our kid, let's get 'em!" Corny struggled to find his own lock key but by the time he had he was locked in the cabin and out of the fight… That didn't narrow the odds.

"'Ere, yo," shouted Eli, "teck yo'r 'onds of that lady's legs, she's mine," and in so saying he sent a perfect right cross straight into the previously unmarked face of one of the pirates.

"My hero," swooned Jessie as she realised that Eli had referred to her as a 'lady'.

Enoch realised that the pirates were using a language he had never heard before, Eli and Jesse were right, it was foreign. He walloped another one sending him flying over the side and into the water, that balanced out the removal of Corny, but they were still in trouble.

One of the pirates, the one who appeared to be in charge suddenly produced a hand gun… He fired it into the air just as Jessie walloped a pirate with the lock key sending him catapulting over the side.

Everyone stopped fighting. The only sound was the splash as Jessie's victim landed in the water

The pirate shouted. "If you do not surrender I will kill you one by one" He leered at Jessie, "I will leave this one 'til last…"

He said this in English but with a heavy foreign accent.

Eli wanted to have a go but Jessie held him back.

"He's got a gun, Eli, this is no time for heroics."

Mushy peas are one thing, but getting shot was something else, three intrepid crew members raised their hands.

"You!" shouted the pirate boss, he was addressing one of his men. "Check the manifest…you know what you are looking for."

"Yo've been doing this longer than me, our kid, what's a manifest, Eli?" whispered Enoch, but the pirate heard him.

"A manifest, my friend is a list of what you are carrying…"

Enoch shook his head, "There ay no manifest, cock, 'cos we knows what we'm carryin', so we doe need a list…"

The pirate frowned, what kind of language is that, is this man some sort of foreigner?

He stepped a little nearer, his gun almost up Enoch's left nostril. "And what would that be, your load I mean?"

"Don't tell 'im, Enoch…." This was Corny, one of the pirates had released him from the cabin.

Ah!" laughed the pirate… "Don't tell him Enoch. Zat can mean only one thing, you do not want me to find out… And zat can only mean one thing…. You are carrying ze mushy peas…. "

He could tell from the expressions on his captives faces he was right.

"Ah, mes amis, eet ees jackpot time…. Search ze boat, destroy ze mushy peas… throw ze barrels into the canal, leave nossink on ze boat.

The gang set to, throwing off the tarpaulins and exposing the precious cargo…

"Ze boss, he will be well pleased, I think," grinned the pirate leader. "Okay, my fine fellows, let us not waste time, throw the barrels overboard and if this motley crew try to stop you, throw zem over as well!"

Just then they all heard a noise, whoopings, hollerings, shoutings and whistlings….even bicycle bells.

"Bloody hell," Enoch took a sharp intake of breath, "It's the cavalry!"

On they came, peddling like fury, coat tails flapping behind them until they reached the battle scene, nearly thirty well-built canal workers all looking for a fight. Not a pretty sight. Abandoning their trusty steeds they clambered aboard President, which while its occupants had been fighting had drifted into the bank; they were brandishing all sorts of weapons, pick axe handles, lump hammers, lock keys…

"Watch it, mates, this one has a gun!" called Corny.

"Not any more he hasn't," answered Boxer-Joe as the pirate leader, pole-axed by one of Boxer's specialities fell on his back in the canal.

"Drag him out, called Eli, we need to ask him some tasty questions…"

"Good point, don't want him to drown, at least not yet."

One Arm took the boat hook off Eli and by hooking it under the pirates collar was able to hold him above water while Chugger and one of the men dragged him ashore.

It was a short-lived fight, with their leader out of it and out-numbered by more than they could work out without pencil and paper the pirates one by one held up their hands in surrender.

The last consignment of mushy peas on the planet was saved…

But.. One Arm had a problem. Why was Jessie here?

"Her auntie in Stourbridge has been took bad and she was asking for Jessie specifically, she might not have long, the poor old gel, so I offered to give Jessie a lift…" Eli was most sincere.

"And there wasn't time to tell you, besides you was somewhere in the yard and I couldn't find you and I was that upset…." Jessie started to cry.

"I told her she could come with me, I would drop her off in Stourbridge and explain to you when I go back, then either myself or one of the boys could bring her back on another trip – probably after the funeral" Eli was still thinking on his feet.

Jessie was still snivelling. "The message was she couldn't hang on long so I thought I would only be away for a few days, I didn't think you would mind, my love."

She snuggled up to the second most important man in her life. One Arm believed every word, the gullible idiot.

"Of course I don't mind…. You must get to Stourbridge as soon as possible… Eli, get Ruby on the move and deliver this young lady to her aunty. Quickly now."

"Yes sir, any second now sir… Come on, miss we have to get you to Stourbridge."

Enoch and Corny were standing listening to this open-mouthed. They both had the same thought, Eli and Jessie, what a double act.

Chugger was also standing watching this dramatic heart-wrenching scene, except unlike One Arm Louis he didn't believe a word of it.. He grinned, good luck to you, Eli my son, he thought, may you enjoy those legs while you can, and let's hope One Arm Louis never finds out Jessie doesn't even have an aunty in Stourbridge.

Oh yes, Jessie's legs were quite famous.

One Arm and Chugger turned their attention to the pirates who were now wondering exactly what was going to happen to them. They had destroyed all the mushy peas in existence apart from the load on President and they had burned down the mushy peas factory not say managed to almost destroy what was left of Chugger Riley's entire business – what was left of it after the groaty pudding scandal…

One of the canal men passed the hand gun to Chugger who checked to see if it was loaded, he could do that, he was in ordnance during the First World War, there was hardly a make of gun he had never handled or fired.

The pirate leader watched as Chugger handled the gun like the expert he was. As quick as a flash Chugger punched the pirate in the throat and as his unfortunate victim opened his mouth to gasp for air he suddenly realised there was a gun barrel wedged in it.

"Neat," whispered Enoch.

"Thank you," grinned Chugger, "just something I picked up in Flanders... Mostly on my own officers who for some reason seemed intent on getting us all killed."

His expression changed, this idiot with the barrel of the hand gun stuck in his gob owed him...

"Who sent you, it's a simple enough question?"

Nothing.. Not a word.

"Oh, I see, a martyr to the cause, well, that suits me."

He grinned and pulled back the hammer, the pirate started shivering.

Nearly there, thought One Arm, who had also had experience with snooty officers in the trenches. Let's hope Chugger knows when to stop, this twat has ruined his business and Chugger doesn't like that.

"I'll ask you again, my son... Who sent you, you have ten seconds."

"How long is ten seconds," whispered Jammy Dodger.

"Ooooh, not very long," answered Enoch, making sure the pirate could hear him. He started counting... Ten... Nine.....eight....seven.... six.... Five..... That was enough.

The unfortunate victim dropped to the floor, his hands held in front of him as if in prayer. His compatriots groaned in disgust.

"Okay... Okay... You win, take ze gun away and I will tell you...."

One Arm took over, bad cop, good cop.

"Now then, my friend, there's nothing to worry about, all we need to know is who is determined to destroy the British mushy peas industry and why... then you and your friends can go free."

And if he believed that, he'd believe anything?

He did believe it

"Francois du Conche."

"Who?"

"Francois du Conche, he is a French chef in Paris, he owns all the best restaurants."

One Arm frowned. "So what, what has owning all the best restaurants got to do….. Oh, I see, he wants to take over the mushy peas industry for himself."

The pirate shook his head… "No, sir, he is determined to destroy your mushy peas industry."

"But why," Chugger was astonished. "We export thousands of tons of mushy peas a year to France, I imagine a lot of that goes to this Francois geezer who is obviously charging top dollar – well it is Paris – and making a fortune. Why destroy it?"

The pirate shrugged his shoulders… "To get rid of the opposition, of course, what else?"

"Opposition to what?" asked One Arm, he still had a problem believing this.

"Opposition to his own business… He has opened his own factory. He is making and marketing '*Petit Pois du Mushez*", an up-market version and he will be able to charge a fortune as it is being made in Paris… It will no longer be ze dish of the Black Country labouring classes it will be ze gourmet delight of the French elite"

Bloody hell, thought Enoch, you couldn't make this up.

"Actually, boys, I told you a little fib" confessed One Arm, "yes, you will be allowed to go back to your loved ones in France, but…. I am asking you as a favour, no I am suggesting…. Er, no actually I am ordering you to volunteer to help re-build the mushy peas factory before you go, under the supervision of some of my boys, of course, we don't want any of you to take an early un-scheduled holiday, do we?"

There was no argument, only forlorn nods of the heads, so One Arm continued.

"It's only fair, after all it was you lot being very inconsiderate and anti-social who burnt it down. Like I said it's only fair." The bad cop took over…. "Like the man said, it's only fair…Then when you have done that you can work for me for six months at the same rate of pay you will get for re-building the mushy peas factory, which in case you were wondering, is nothing…. Oh, we will feed and house you, you can sleep in one of the sheds and you can eat all the mushy peas you want."

What was there to argue about, the pirates were licked and they knew it.

Except the pirate leader wanted to say something, he raised his hand a little.

Chugger smiled. Yes, mon brave, what is it?

"Monsieur… When we don't get back to Paris on time Francois du Conche he will come looking for us."

Chugger chuckled, "I am glad you said that, I would like a word with this Francois geezer, because he is going to take out a contract with me for two thousand gallons of mushy peas delivered over the next year – cash in advance, of course."

The pirate chief shrugged. "And if he doesn't?"

"Then he will be the first person in the history of the world – as far as we know - to be buried alive in a barrel of mushy peas."

That pretty much put an end to it. The mushy peas factory was re-built, with the pirates help of course, then they worked for Chugger for six months before five of them eventually went home, two of them liked it in Tipton so much they asked if they could stay. Actually one of them was employed as mate when Enoch got his first canal boat.

"Mind you," announced Enoch to his new crew, "you will have to go when I find a female member of the human race to crew for me."

The man was French, he understood.

The owner of the mushy peas factory wanted to ask One Arm Louis exactly why a load of French gangsters had volunteered to help out but at the last minute refrained, he thought that maybe it was best he didn't know.

Francois du Conche didn't put in an appearance, somehow the pirate leader loyal to the last had managed to get word back to Paris and warned him not to come, although he did warn Francois of the consequences of not doing what Chugger Riley had said, otherwise he wouldn't need a coffin for his funeral, so Francois did the only thing he could do, he accepted delivery of the contracted amount of mushy peas as directed by Chugger, cash in advance, and not one of his restaurants was ever vandalised... See below.

Chugger had never actually said so in public - although he had hinted to the pirate leader knowing that the information would somehow get to France - but it is believed by most of those involved in this mushy peas affair that had Francois reneged on the deal with Chugger his restaurants would have received the same treatment as the mushy peas factory.

If asked, Chugger would have 'tut-tutted' and denied every word.

Chugger's own boys were disappointed when Francois agreed to the deal, they had been looking forward to the trip, most of them hadn't been to France since the war and to go in peacetime knowing that they were guaranteed to come home would have been a novelty.

Eli and Jessie spent a happy couple of days in Stourbridge, and believe it or not, her auntie made a full recovery...
It was a miracle.
After all, as Eli pointed out, you never know when you might want her to be at death's door again do you!?

The Enoch and Eli Trilogy

Ending with

The Strange Affair of the Pork Scratching Drought.

Peter Yates

This final story I have to tell you about took place long before
the two stories you have just read, in fact this tale took place
before the onset of the First World War. I have long wondered
what folks would have thought had they known that five years
or so after this saga the country would be engulfed in war and
millions of its sons would be lost for ever. Like I say I have
long wondered but many times I wish I hadn't.
We are talking about the Edwardian period, Queen Victoria
had passed on in January 1901 and we had a new monarch,
King Edward. It started the era known to historians as the
'Belle Epoque', the beautiful period, maybe that should have
given us a clue as to what was to follow just a few short years
down the line, they always say don't they that good and bad
follow each other in a kind of rotation.
Yes, this pre-dates the previous two stories, it took place even
before Enoch and Eli had found their new lives on the canals
and before Eli found his new love, Jessie, who had vacated a
gas lamp to be with her hero.
In fact at the time of the pork scratching drought both Enoch
and Eli were still of school age, they even went to school on
the odd occasion when they weren't needed to scratch a penny
or two doing odd jobs to help the family budget.
Their parents – Wilf and Prudence, known to all as Pru - were
involved in the same business as many at that time, especially
in the Tipton area, that is they made pork scratchings. This
work was mostly done in the wash house down the yard

where the brine was mixed – I am honour bound to not tell you the process, it being, even now, a closely guarded secret. They were all family businesses, many a back yard was devoted to the production of pork scratchings which were sent in little packets nationwide, to pretty much every up-market pub – and a good few down-market ones come to think of it - in the land in fact and all points overseas sewn up in hessian sacks. Oh yes, it was big business. It was said at the time that the newly emerging railways of the midlands would have been far less prosperous had the pork scratching trade not existed, unimpeded access to the seaports was a necessity. In the manner of Willenhall a few miles away where there was a lock and key workshop at the back of almost every dwelling so it was in the pork scratching triangle, a name given it by outsiders and covered an area between Tipton, Bilston and Coseley, although there were pork scratching producers outside this area of course, but the vast majority were inside this geographical triangle.

I have been told they don't teach this in schools any-more - local history, that is - which is a national disgrace, I don't see why every school child should be force fed the locations of the coal mines of Brazil where they are never likely to visit on an away-day week-end but never the wonders and history of their own region, where they could pop round on their bikes and have a look, it is such a shame.

It was just before Christmas in nineteen twelve I think it must have been when the tragedy struck, a tragedy brought about by and large by government policy it has to be said.
It was some snooty government minister, you know the sort, guaranteed income, guaranteed pension, guaranteed expense account and guaranteed to never have to do any work who noticed it first. The peasants were making too much money, too much meaning a copper or two above the breadline.

In fact he noticed that there were working class families who earned in a week almost as much as he spent – and when dining with a colleague discussing which race meeting to attend that afternoon he could claim it was a business arrangement which qualified for him to get his money back, obviously – on a good – and long - lunch at his club. Governments throughout modern history have always known that if you want to maintain control of the masses keep said masses short of two things, the truth courtesy of the BBC current affairs channels, and disposable income by increasing the rate of VAT every now and again: that way you can promise the earth but blame outside influences - the weather destroying the crops therefore increasing the amount of subsidy payable to the poor destitute farmers ruling out any increase in the minimum wage this year – sorry, folks, we can't do both, the cost of maintaining the fleet of government ministers limousines which of course has to be replaced every time a new model comes out, it's image you see, can't risk being accused of being 'so last year'; a demand for more cash from the EU or a dictatorship somewhere demanding an increase in the overseas aid programme because he needs a new yacht. Which of course has no bearing on the salaries and expenses of the ruling classes – of all parties - they who make the rules, and making the rules in your favour is easy when you have had generations of practice and over the generations this practice has been honed to perfection.

Like I say, this twit saw the danger signs, if the populace were picking up too much money, the next thing is they will develop a big mouth and start demanding their rights.

Rights…? They are the working class, what gives them the right to have rights?

The answer was simple - it was in fact a twofold answer. Make sure the peasantry didn't earn enough to feel comfortable about getting too big for their boots – those who could afford boots - and at the same time do the government a bit of good as a bonus.

It didn't take long, this had to be nipped in the bud, and quickly.

They rushed through a bill in parliament – claiming a national emergency - not only bunging a high rate of purchase tax on pork scratchings but to add insult to injury the producers were going to have to pay a duty in the manner of the alcohol industry. Every hessian sack of scratchings to be sent overseas attracted a heavy export duty almost equivalent to the purchase price of the sack itself.

Well, it doesn't need a university degree to work it out, orders dried up, foreign consumers, those in the diners of New York for example refused to pay such exorbitant prices and American importers cancelled their orders, as did those from Japan, China and the Philippines.

Street corner bars in other countries, but only those with a small British ex-pat population managed to keep a few orders going and only because of the nostalgia value to their Brit patrons until one day when the export duty went up one too many times and even they stopped buying. As happens on so many occasions when the British government gets involved and thinks it can see a wind-fall profit, it gets too greedy and inevitably kills off the goose that was quite happily laying the golden eggs.

It was a drought, a veritable drought.

The pork scratching industry collapsed, it was a national disaster. Questions in the House, calls for the government to resign, they of course refused, it wasn't their fault they said if folks couldn't afford to buy that rubbish. Besides, they now had to find something else with which they could bleed the populace dry before finally taxing it out of existence, a working class something else, of course, nothing important. Couldn't afford to buy that rubbish….? Another demand for heads to roll, this time from the Liberal party who although wouldn't be seen dead eating pork scratchings themselves decided that it wouldn't do their image any harm if they stuck up for those that do. But of course, no-one resigned, the gravy train rolled on, its passengers totally unmoved by the trials and tribulations of those out there in the real world.

The devastation this pork scratching drought brought about was... well, devastating.

Whole streets closed their doors on the wash houses down the yard for good, except on Mondays when the lady of the house, pork scratchings or no pork scratchings had to do the washing. The fact that the washing was done in the same copper tub with the coal fire underneath it to bring it to the boil as well as the boiling of the brine for the pork scratchings the rest of the week had never given any bother, on the contrary there were those who maintained that it was this extra something from wash day – the residue from the washing powder, perhaps – that gave the pork scratchings from the triangle that extra piquancy – and therefore higher sales - never found in pork scratchings made elsewhere.

But all that was yesterday, the wash house boilers remained cold for six days a week, the bags of salt piled up in the corner melted into an ooze before going hard having soaked up the condensation generated by wash day, and the raw ingredients that were now destined to never be made into scratchings themselves - the main ingredient in fact – that had been left hanging around in onion sacks from hooks dangling from the wash house roof when the orders dried up had to be eaten by the very ones who would normally have been turning the raw meat into the well-known delicacy, other-wise it would have gone rotten and therefore a total right-off.

Some families continued to produce a limited quantity of pork scratchings for themselves, on the quiet, of course, if only to use up the raw meat stored in the wash house, they figured that as long as they were producing only for their own consumption they weren't breaking the law, but even then they couldn't eat it quickly enough to save some from going off.

Many a housewife came up with several brand new recipes in order to use up the raw ingredient that should have been a bag of scratchings… After all, with no money coming in there was nothing else to eat.

The newly impoverished introduced the fast going off slivers of raw pig to a plateful of sprouts, boiled beetroot stuffed with scratchings, carrot and scratching pie and one particular favourite mashed swede and/or turnip and scratching compote, all easy to grow on the allotment. The ladies of the house wrapped these otherwise boring ingredients in a rough pastry but as supplies ran out very often it was simply swede or carrot pie with a hint of scratchings to give it some crunch for supper.

But inevitably, even that source of nourishment dried up, or became simply inedible because the pork skins had sat in the wash house for weeks on end, soaking up the atmosphere finally tasting like a Reckitt's blue bag.

After only a short period of time it was no longer possible to hear the plaintive cry that had rung out over the industrial landscape for weeks almost every dinner time - "Oh God, not bloody scratchings and chips again!"

The pork scratching triangle had never known such hardship, indeed it is difficult to describe such horror, not since Victorian times had there been such poverty.

Something had to be done – but not by the ruling classes who were quite happy with the situation, the peasants, half-starved and skint were subdued and the extra income from the export duty and purchase tax, for a while at least, had covered parliamentary expenses for several months without those necessary items of everyday living – for a member of parliament that is - being a run on the national purse.

But…. and ignored by government ministers who were complacent in their feeling of superiority, in almost every front parlour in the pork scratching triangle there were the rumblings of discontent.

Something had to be done…..but no-one knew what!

Except maybe Enoch and Eli's father Wilf…………………

The Fight-back Begins

It happened on one particular Monday, the date immaterial but it was a momentous day, a historic day, this was the day when at approximately nine thirty in the morning immediately after breakfast had they been able to afford some Enoch and Eli's mother declared that they were six weeks behind with the rent, thirty three bob in all and the rent man would be coming that afternoon, so that made it seven. Not at all funny, they had never been behind with the rent since the day she and Wilf got married fifteen years ago, and the rent man had only allowed them this latitude – six weeks – on the strength that up until now they had been model tenants. But even the rent man was under pressure, most of his tenants were behind with the rent and most of those stood no chance of getting back up to date unless the man of the house could find a job, and that wasn't going to be easy, the only trade most of them knew was the delicate art of scratching production, a skill not easily transferable to anything else.

"Six weeks arrears going on seven, we have to do something, Wilf or we'll be out on the street, or worse, in the spare bedroom at my mother's, and I'd have to leave behind my nearly new gas stove which would be a disaster 'cos it ay paid for yet, good job it's only one and a tanner a week, any more and the gas board would have to come and take it back."

Wilf smiled, he wasn't worried, he had worked out exactly what they were going to do, he had been thinking about what they were going to do for weeks whilst working in the allotment. He had honed his plans to perfection and now while the family was together and his wife Pru was panicking about having to go back and live with her mother was the ideal time to make the announcement.

"Don't worry about it, lass, 'cos we are going to do something about it, I have a plan."

I'll bet you do, thought Pru a trifle sarcastically, although she wouldn't dare say it out loud. Being out of work and having the pork scratching business effectively taken away through the exorbitant taxes hadn't done her hubby's confidence a bit of good; Wilf had been one of the best pork scratching makers in the business, a top man, he was well known for it, his nickname, 'The Scratching King' wasn't for nothing, but since the crash he hadn't been able to get used to being idle and out of work, or as he would put it, useless. It was his job as hunter gatherer to feed his family but because he could no longer do that even for reasons beyond his control – which made it worse - it hurt, a lot.

Pru stood and folded her arms across her ample bosom, which in the old days when they could afford it and Wilf was late back from the pub it usually meant okay then, let's hear it, but make it good.

"Okay, then… what is this master plan?"

Wilf smiled, possibly the first time for months.

"We are going into the pork scratching business."

Enoch, Eli and their mother Pru exchanged worried looks, since the collapse of the pork scratching industry other families had experienced this, the head of the household losing it and going gaga; like many of them, some close friends, Wilf was one small step away from two men in white coats and a van with a lock on the back door turning up to take him away.

Pru was solicitous she sat on the arm of his chair, she was worried.

"It's okay, love, we are here, we will look after you, yo've had a bad dream that's all."

Wilf shrugged her off and stood with his back to where there should be a fire except they couldn't afford the coal.

"I'm not going loopy, love, I mean it, we are going back into the pork scratching business…. Both Joe from the Royal Oak and Eric from The Prince have told me that if we can produce scratchings again, just us, no-one else – they both know we were the best in the business - they will buy every packet and sell them to their customers from under the counter, no purchase tax, no duty, no questions asked… a kind of bootleg scratching."

Pru went cold, this would be illegal, de-frauding the revenue men was a major crime…. But having to live in one room at her mother's was a worse one.

"Listen," Wilf continued, "While I have been on the allotment I have been working it out, we make the pork scratchings in the wash house just like the old days, we are lucky, no-one else has to use our wash house, there's only thee, so no-one need know what we are doing."

He was gaining in confidence. "Enoch and Eli will deliver the scratchings to the two pubs – and maybe more pubs if word gets round - on Grandad Frank's old butcher's bike, it has been lying in the shed doing nothing since he passed over…If challenged, and I feel that's very unlikely, who is going to accuse two young boys of smuggling scratchings, Enoch and Eli can say they are going down the allotment to pick up some veggies for Sunday dinner."

No-one was arguing….. yet, so Wilf crossed his fingers and carried on.

"The scratchings can be carried in the wicker basket on the front of the bike and covered over sort of quite nonchalantly with an old raincoat, in case it rains – to keep the veggies dry, if someone asks - all completely innocent."

There was still no comment from his open-mouthed family.

"Both Joe and Eric have told me they will pay me in advance every week – they are just as keen as me, 'cos their business is suffering with no scratchings to sell, folks with a dry salty mouth buy more ale, but folks who ay got a dry and salty mouth doe, so Joe and Eric ay selling as much ale as they'd like, it's as simple as that. Paying me in advance means we can pop round the abattoir for the raw materials on a Monday morning, the Co-op for the salt and maybe a bit of bacon and an egg or two for ourselves and still have enough to start paying off the rent, if there's any left we can have fish and chips on a Friday just like the old days; we can start by paying off a couple of weeks rent, we had better not try to pay off more than that for the moment, it might raise the question 'where did they get the money from?' My way, if anyone starts asking questions we can say your mother has helped us out knowing full well that no-one is going to say anything to her she is such a fire-breathing old dragon they wouldn't dare risk getting their eyebrows singed."

Wilf slumped down on his chair, he needed a Woodbine but hadn't been able to afford to buy any cigarettes for weeks.

For better or worse he had dropped his bombshell....

Hell, he was nervous.

The room stayed silent for ages, Wilf thought maybe he had made a mistake, he had wondered to himself on many an occasion whilst brooding about it in the shed on the allotment whether it was the right thing to do or not... But, what else had they got? The answer was simple, a big fat nothing.

Pru paced up and down – well, as far as you can pace in a titchy little parlour. She went out through the back door and spent ages staring out over the wall at the cemetery.....

Enoch and Eli were getting excited although it would have been a mistake to show it, they were going to be gun-runners or illicit booze smugglers except it would be pork scratchings, but the principle is the same thing. They would be delivering pork scratchings right under the noses of the cops and the revenue men, how exciting is that?

Finally Pru came back in poured a cup of tea and sat down, her expression told them nothing, there were goose pimples all up her arm; she stared in amazement at her husband, she had never known until this fateful morning that this normally quite timid man sitting in front of her staring at her with those big brown eyes she had fallen in love with all those years ago was a tiger in disguise prepared to risk everything including his own freedom in order to feed his family and pay the rent, she felt very proud, very scared, but very proud.

A vision of the back bedroom at her mother's house flashed through her mind. She knew what she had to do and that was either support her husband or start packing... No, she would be prepared to anything but move back to her mother's.

She slowly nodded her head. "It would be a risk, Wilf, in fact it would be the biggest risk we have ever undertaken, I hope you realise that."

Wilf also nodded, he managed another smile. "Of course I do, my love, but without wishing to cause offence have you got any better ideas?"

The vision of the back bedroom at her mother's once again reared its ugly head.

Pru smiled, "no offence taken, my darling because no, I haven't and yes you are right.... Okay, we'll do it."

Wilf started breathing again.

Pru turned her full attention on Enoch and Eli, her facial expression was the one that said, listen to me and don't argue.

"Now listen to me, you two, we are going to give this a go, your father has come up with a brilliant although very risky idea, if we get caught he will almost certainly go to prison for a very long time and we don't want that, do we?"

They shook their heads.

"So... You will promise me here and now that you will not mention one word of what we intend to do to a living soul."

"Not even your grandma," added Wilf.

"Especially not your grandma," stressed Pru.

Enoch and Eli were far from thick, they knew the score, they knew that while the forthcoming adventure was – for them at least – something to look forward to, if they blabbed to anyone, even a mate at school, the whole pack of cards would almost certainly collapse around their ears and it might be years before they saw their father again, especially if as they suspected they still sent convicts to Australia.

Enoch as the eldest took the lead. Solemnly he placed one hand on his heart.

"We promise, don't we our kid, we won't breathe a word, not even to gran."

Eli placed one hand on his heart, or where he thought his heart was, Enoch moved his brother's hand to the other side of his chest, Wilf resisted the urge to giggle.

"It's a promise," announced Eli, in his most solemn voice, "not a word will we utter, not to no-one, alive or dead, and if we break our promise you can send us to Sunday school every Sunday for a whole year as punishment."

Wow, that was some vow.

Do you know what, thought Pru, I feel better already.

All went well enough, Wilf scooted off round to 'The Prince' and 'The Royal Oak' from where as promised he collected his first week's money in advance, then, trying not to look like the cat that got the cream – any happy expression would have stood out like a boil on the backside, everyone was so miserable these days – he trotted off to the abattoir to pay for a week's supply of raw meat, promising that his two boys would be calling later that day with their bike for collection. He had promised both licensees that they would take delivery of their very first pork scratchings for months in time for the Saturday lunchtime darts match. The arrangement was if any of the punters asked where the scratchings had come from they would be told to shut their gob or they wouldn't be in the team next week; and anyway they were made in Japan from Vietnamese pot-bellied pigs and if they blabbed and put an end to the deliveries the rest of the customers would be told who did the blabbing and retribution would be swift and complete behind the men's toilets out the back.

Talking about the bike, Enoch and Eli managed to drag it out of the shed where it had languished ever since Granddad Frank had passed over; it was covered with old tarpaulins and all kinds of junk. Actually when they managed to get it out into the daylight it didn't look too bad, the tyres still had some air in them which meant the rubber hadn't perished and apart from the rust on the wheel rims and the handlebars it looked pretty tidy.

"We can soon get this looking like new our kid," announced Eli.

Enoch shook his head, he didn't think so.

"It'll only take a bit of hard work, listen Enoch, our dad is risking everything I think it's only fair that we do our bit and polishing up this old bike, to me, is part of that."

Enoch smiled, "that's not why I shook my head.... If we clean this up too much it will attract too much attention and that we can't afford, all we need to do is make it road-worthy, polish some of the rust off the wheels, wash out the basket on the front and maybe rub a duster over the frame, that way when folks see us out on the streets they won't have the excuse to stop us so that they can admire our bike and have a nosy look in the basket to see if they can blag a couple of carrots."

Eli whistled, "yo'm a genius, our kid, I day think of that."

Enoch grinned, "yo will when yo'm as old as me."

Wilf arrived back home delighted with his morning's work so far. He proudly presented his wife with enough hard cash to buy something to eat – nothing too extravagant, don't want folks to start thinking – and enough cash to pay off two weeks rent that afternoon when the rent man came calling, was he going to get a surprise. Pru was to tell him that as long as he kept his trap shut she would pay him two weeks every week until the arrears were paid off and he was to mention this to no-one, especially her mother.

Full force of the Law

It must have been about three months or maybe four when the illicit pork scratching operation almost came to nought.
Things had been going swimmingly, no problems whatsoever, the pork scratchings were up to Wilf's own exacting standards – he was an artist – and the punters at 'The Royal Oak' and 'The Prince' were delighted that they could once again buy pork scratchings, there was no hint of anyone asking tricky questions, there was a ready supply and that was all they wanted to know. There were a few who wondered at the legality of it but who cares, an illegal scratching is better than no scratching at all.
By the end of the first month the rent was up to date although as far as the neighbours were concerned – and Pru's mother – times were still hard.
One Monday morning Wilf was accepting his order and one week's money in advance from Joe at 'The Royal Oak' when Joe grinned and handed over a piece of paper.
"What's this, mate?" asked Wilf.
All the piece of paper had on it was the name 'Cock and Bull' St Anne's Road.
"Albert at 'The Cock and Bull' wants pork scratchings, Wilf, same arrangement as me and Eric."
Wilf didn't know whether to smile or panic, someone had blabbed, someone had told Albert from 'The Cock and Bull' that he was making bootleg scratchings.
"It's okay, Wilf, your secret is safe, I told Albert that the supplier would deliver to me and he could collect them from here, that way there's still only Eric and me who knows what's going on."

Clever thinking, thought Wilf, I can't see a problem with that, so he readily agreed. Albert would give the cash in advance to Joe, who would pay this over to Wilf at the same time as paying for his own delivery, Wilf would deliver both orders to Joe, then Joe would hand over the scratchings when Albert called for them on the Saturday morning and everyone's a winner.

Can't go wrong…. Oh yes it can…. but not yet.

Albert's brother-in-law, Ken, at 'The Horse and Jockey' spotted the scratchings behind the bar of 'The Cock and Bull' when he called in to borrow a crate of light ale.

He insisted on a delivery of scratchings for his own pub. Albert explained that as it was illegal it was a slick operation run on a need to know basis, and he had no idea of the source of the pork scratchings stressing that actually neither he nor Ken needed to know where the illicit scratchings were coming from as long as they turned up on time and in any case it is best not to ask questions, walls have ears and the revenue men could be anywhere and what you don't know you can't tell them should they catch you. Oh yes, and it was cash in advance.

Agreeing to this secrecy Ken left some money with Albert for a delivery of scratchings, Albert took the money to Joe at 'The Royal Oak' who gave it to Wilf who sent Enoch and Eli with their butcher's bike to 'The Royal Oak' with the extra scratchings on board. The basket on the front of the bike was getting increasingly heavier and heavier every Saturday morning that went by.

Gretchen at 'The Red Bull' heard that her rivals were selling bootleg scratchings – somehow the word had got around, it was never going to remain a close kept secret for long – and at the next licensed victuallers meeting she tackled Eric the landlord of 'The Prince', who of course denied all knowledge. She cornered Albert giving him the full frontal of her behind the bar blouse, he managed to blag his way out of that sending Gretchen off to see Joe who, if you are managing to follow this was landlord of 'The Royal Oak'.

Now Joe was the only one who –apart from Eric –knew where the scratchings were coming from and he was honour bound to keep schtum.

"I'm not saying Gretch, yes, I know who makes them but I am never going to tell you nor anybody else. I've been doing very well out of the deal and I am not going to risk losing money by blabbing to thee."

"I ay asking yo to blab, you bloody old fool, all I am asking is, when yo gets yo'r own 'cos get some for me?"

That's different, and so it came to pass that there was one extra pub to supply…..

Easy peasy…. oh no it isn't.

The very next Saturday morning and Enoch and Eli set off from the wash house with their butcher's bike… In the basket on the front was a consignment of scratchings for 'The Royal Oak', another for 'The Prince', a third for 'The Cock and Bull', yet another for 'The Horse and Jockey', and finally another for 'The Red Bull'.

It was hard going, ideally they should have taken two trips but Wilf had been concerned whether someone might been a little too curious seeing two boys and a butcher's bike go round the back of a public house twice in one morning, both times with a bulging basket on the front but both times when they came back into sight nothing in the basket except for an old army greatcoat. On this particular and fateful morning the bike was top-heavy there was that much weight in the basket. For once they couldn't free-wheel down bug-hole bridge with their feet on the handle bars, it needed all their skill to keep the damn thing upright…

And that was when it happened, the near-calamity, although at the time no-one realised that it could have been a calamity.

Minding their own business they were passing the gates to old Mister Thomas's coalyard, when the aforesaid Mister Thomas as usual drove his horse and cart out of the gate as usual without looking, just as Enoch and Eli were passing singing 'roll out the barrel' at the tops of their voices, the horse shied, raised itself on its back legs and shed fifteen hundred weight of nutty slack all over the cobbles, and because of the excess weight on the front end of the bike Enoch and Eli lost control, the bike tipped sideways shedding its load on top of the nutty slack, hundreds of little paper bags everywhere.

Apart from Eli getting a grazed knee – which he managed to get several times a week anyway - the two boys came to no harm although Enoch did have to roll pretty urgently to one side as the horse's front hooves came back to earth just missing Enoch's head as they clattered and skidded on the cobbles.

Passers-by helped of course – well, folks did in those days – and pretty soon with no harm done Enoch and Eli were on their way.

Did I say 'with no harm done'?

The next Tuesday afternoon was a Tuesday to never forget.

Wilf was, as usual up to his neck in brine and scratchings, stirring away at the old copper boiler, weaving his magic.

He sensed something more than saw....

He turned to the door which was always open due to the heat and steam from the copper.

And there facing him in the open doorway watching everything Wilf was doing was another kind of copper, Sergeant Wilson from the local cop shop.

The cheeky beggar even saluted.

"Morning, Wilf, busy I see."

"Mmmmm…Mmmmmm.Mmmmmm." was all Wilf could say.

"Thought so," smiled the big burly sergeant. "The word was you were brewing up something special – and illegal, and it looks like they were right."

To bring the reader up to date someone had noticed that one of the paper bags that had spilled on to the road the previous Saturday morning when Enoch, Eli and their trusty butcher's bike had fallen out with the coalman's horse had split open revealing its contents – without doubt bootleg scratchings. This violently anti-social person had pocketed the evidence and rushed round the police station and snitched, hence the unwelcome visit from Sergeant Wilson, who produced the ripped paper bag as evidence, Wilf noticed that someone had eaten the contents.

"Sorry, Wilf, but there it is, yo've been catched. Sorry."

The game was up, it had been fun and they had paid off the rent but now they had to take the consequences.

"It's a fair cop, Sergeant, lock me up…."

Sergeant Wilson grinned, "Doe be daft Wilf, I ay gonna lock thee up…"

The sergeant looked around the wash house and found a chair, he sat and made himself comfortable.

"Now then Wilf, I want you to listen and listen good… I have been authorised by the catering committee of the nick to come and see you to ask – no, demand – that providing you supply us with fifty bags of scratchings a week, for free of course, no charge, no further action will be taken vis a vis the incident on Saturday and the untimely and unfortunate discovery of your bootleg scratchings operation, by a vigilant and socially-minded sergeant, meaning me, meaning right here and now will conveniently be forgotten."

Wilf was open-mouthed. The sergeant continued.

"The Inspector has instructed me to tell thee that if yo agree no-one need know and the nasty little oik who blabbed and snitched will be told to shut their gob or they will be arrested and charged with the theft of the paper bag and its contents, 'cos we noticed it was almost empty….."

The sergeant waited, then he continued,

"Wilf, we all know yo'm only tryin' yo'r best for the family, yo ay doin' no real 'arm, but I cor say as we'll be able to keep thee out of trouble if the revenue men catches thee, they'm pretty much above the law themselves, or as the inspector says, they make it up as they go along, and if yo agree I've been authorised by the inspector to tell thee yo wo 'ear no more about Saturday's episode with the coalmon's 'oss. How many times we wull be able to cover for you I don't know, but as long as we keep gettin' free scratchings we'll certainly do us best, am I making myself clear. But, 'avin' said that, if the revenue men get too hot we will deny all knowledge of thee and the scratchings."

That evening Wilf reported to his family exactly what Sergeant Wilson had proposed, and that he had readily agreed. Pru initially had the same reaction as her husband, that they had been dropped in it upside down feet first, but after a little thought she also realised, as had Wilf, that this meant that effectively – and up to a point - they had police protection. Although….. she also wanted to know why Enoch and Eli had been careless enough to leave the evidence lying around in the street the day of the confrontation with the cart horse.

"Cos we day want to be trampled on by 'is bloody great hooves, mother, that 'orse was clatterin' around doin' 'is best to find my 'ead," answered Enoch. "I ay surprised we left a bag or two behind, we was lucky part of us day get left behind, squashed into the cobbles!"

Prue nodded, that was fair comment.

"The point is," broke in Wilf, "We have got away with it, all we have to do is give the cops a few bags for free and nothing else will be done about it."

After this initial and potentially dangerous scare things managed to continue on an upward trend, in fact it was so good Enoch and Eli had to scour the town for a larger and more efficient mode of transport, finally electing for a trolley that Jimmy Hancock's' father had built for him to fasten behind his bike to carry all his tackle when he went fishing, but as lads are Jimmy went off fishing when he discovered Thelma Williams' far more appealing tackle and was glad to swap the trolley for several copies of Health and Efficiency which Enoch had previously traded for a shoe box full of glass alley marbles.

The great unveiling of the new delivery vehicle took place in the yard behind the houses, Enoch proudly at the helm, Eli sitting on the plank stretched across the side walls of the trolley. They pointed out to their parents that when the locals had got used to seeing them out and about they wouldn't even dream that there was room for oodles of bags of scratchings hiding under the plank as well as the usual ones in the basket on the front of the butcher's bike.

And they had thought of this all by themselves.

There were never two more proud parents.

By the end of the second trading quarter they had picked up seven more pubs, three working men's clubs, one conservative club and the Masonic Hall all desperately needing pork scratchings in ever increasing quantities.

It was inevitable that folks would discover that almost half the licensed premises at this end of the town were selling bootleg scratchings, but any thoughts of breaking in on this illicit trade was tempered with the knowledge that the local nick was also a receiver of the pork scratchings and would therefore have no truck with anyone trying to muscle in on whoever was supplying them; not that Wilf would have minded actually, trade was so brisk he was having trouble keeping up with the orders and he made it quite clear that for the moment at least he could not supply anyone else.

What a change from only a few short months previously when they had been scared out of their wits expecting any moment to be turfed out of their home because they were so far behind with the rent.

The revenue men knew something was up, they had scoured the town to no avail, nothing. But, being of the unimaginative type and programmed to persist they carried on looking and listening.

It was shortly after the big boss in London decided to have a change in personnel when the wheels became a trifle wobbly on Wilf's pork scratching business.

And it was simple how it happened.

One of the new revenue men, as did they all, went into several pubs one Saturday night, it wasn't such a bad job, especially as all booze bought was on expenses – and when he went into the public bar of 'The Prince' he asked for a pint of Bank's. The barmaid, new to the job asked him if he wanted anything else, he looked down her top and smiled.

"What have you got?" he asked, after all the rest of the evening was free he had been in his allotted seven pubs.

"Well…" she smiled back, he's not bad looking she thought. "If you promise not to tell, I have a special treat."

The night looks promising, thought the revenue man.

"I'm in, miss, I'll have whatever you are willing to give me." How did he get this lucky?

She smiled again, "I'm not giving it to you, you cheeky devil, yo'll have to pay."

Showing rather more than her mother would approve of she bent down, giving him a quick look – as he thought – of the delights to come after closing time, and produced from under the bar – no, not her bra, pay attention - a bag of pork scratchings.

Pure gold dust……

Blowing on his whistle to rattle up reinforcements he shot to the door and barred the exit.

"Everybody stay exactly where you are." He flashed his badge, "I am a government agent and you are all under suspicion of having in your possession one or more bags of illegally brewed pork scratchings."

As if from nowhere several bags of scratchings were thrown in great haste into the fire; the evidence that connected the punters to the crime was destroyed, but not the evidence still hiding behind the bar.

Eric, the landlord, hearing the commotion ran in from the snug to see the revenue man standing triumphantly in front of him flashing his badge of office.

"You, sir, are under arrest, anything you say will be completely ignored."

The game was up, the word went round faster than a dose of castor oil, every bag of scratchings behind every bar was destroyed in the flames, there was nothing to link the other landlords, much to their relief, but Eric was catched.

In no time at all the revenue men had all the information they needed, the source of the supply, the dubious part-time protection from the police, certain members of which the revenue men intended to sort out later, which came as no surprise and of course the address of the 'factory'. But still….Fifty bags of free scratchings a week and for what, nothing? At least Sergeant Wilson popped round after all the dust had settled to apologise saying that the inspector had denied all knowledge and he – the sergeant - had been advised to do the same, the question of pension rights seemed to weigh in the conversation with the inspector rather heavily.

Triumphantly and rather mob-handed they swooped on Wilf on the Monday morning when he was just firing up the boiler ready to make this week's supply.

He never made it; very roughly – the revenue men didn't have to abide by the same rules as the regular law-enforcement agencies as they worked directly for a government department – they handcuffed Wilf and searched the wash house for evidence, which as it was Monday and Wilf had only just come back from the abattoir with fresh supplies they found in abundance.

What could he say, nothing, so he saved his defence.

Let Justice Prevail

What Pru and the boys couldn't understand was why Wilf was acting so unconcerned, almost as if he hadn't a care in the world. Even as the court case drew near he was so casual it was unreal.
He hadn't even given up making the scratchings, he made a new batch every week storing them in the coal shed for delivery when the court case was over. He didn't supply any of his normal outlets during this time because quite frankly they were a load of wusses and wouldn't take the risk, but undaunted Wilf was preparing for better times to come.

"Wilfred Terence Wood, you are charged with the manufacturing and supply of illicit pork scratchings from your place of residence, illicit because your production is with the express intent of defrauding his majesties government of the duties imposed on said pork scratchings by their democratic process.. How do you plead?"
They were the opening words at his trial. He stood proud as a peacock in the dock, never once fearing to outstare the clerk of the court as the charge was read out. Pru and as it was a school holiday, the boys, sat in the public gallery and feared the worst.
"Not guilty Your Honour," the words rang out confident and clear, he made certain he didn't drop the 'H' in honour.
Pru frowned, how can he plead not guilty, he was caught bang to rights, the scratchings were all over the wash house floor and he had brine up to his armpits.
The Counsel for the Prosecution rose.
"If My Lord pleases?"
The judge nodded, this wasn't going to take long, he knew the evidence was stacked up against this man in the dock, so golf was a definite prospect for the afternoon.

"Mister Wood, you have heard the charge against you and you have chosen to plead not guilty, I put it to you that the prosecution intends to show quite clearly that there is more than enough evidence to convict you ten times over, what do you say to that?"

Wilf smiled and answered quietly and with consummate confidence.

"With no offence intended to you personally, sir, I put it to you you do not have any evidence whatsoever that I have been making pork scratchings."

The Council for the prosecution stepped forward and pointed to a large table in the middle of the courtroom the top of which was piled high with packets of pork scratchings, all packed in the brand new white paper bags with the new logo proudly printed on the front that had only been delivered the day before the 'bust'. Wilf had sat up all that night packing the pork scratchings in their new bags much to Pru's disgust, she tried to argue but Wilf was adamant that it was necessary. All he said was "Trust me."

She did trust him, wasn't it due to his idea followed by his hard work that they had paid the rent man and generally got them out of the mire? She said no more.

Wilf had said that because the business was doing well the product should be marketed to its best advantage, so these new packets had been the order of the day. Pru had even argued that it was an unnecessary expense but Wilf had insisted. "Trust me," he was smiling when he said it.

Prosecution cleared his throat, although in his opinion this case wasn't going to last long enough to get a sore throat.

"Mister Wood, on the table before us we can see exhibit one through to exhibit three thousand and twenty seven in no particular order. Packets of pork scratchings recovered from your wash house. I put it to you that you are guilty of making these pork scratchings we see before us and distributing them in such a way that you intended to defraud His Majesty's government of revenue courtesy of the duty imposed by Parliament."

Wilf didn't flinch, Enoch and Eli were so proud.

"And I put it to you, sir, that I am not guilty of defrauding anyone of the exorbitant duty imposed by this government on the manufacture and distribution of pork scratchings!"

"You tell 'im, dad!" shouted Eli.

"Silence!" the judge banged his gavel.

Eli giggled, Pru gave him a clout on the back of his head – but not hard enough to knock his cap off.

The judge saw and approved.

Pru shook her head, what is Wilf playing at?

The prosecution persisted.

"In front of us are three thousand and twenty seven reasons why you are guilty; Mister Wood I put it to you that I think it is time you changed your plea to guilty and throw yourself on the mercy of the court.... We have established that prior to this unfortunate affair you have always been a model citizen but you were drawn into this tragic business purely because of your desire to do what was best for your family for which we commend you. For that the court will be merciful I am sure. I put it to you that you change your plea."

Throw yourself on the mercy of the court, willed Pru.... Do it.

"I put it to you that I am changing nothing. I am not guilty of the manufacture and distribution of pork scratchings, neither am I guilty of attempting to evade duties imposed, however harshly on said products by those who believe themselves to be mightier than we. Neither do I need the mercy of the court, but thank you very much for the kind thought."

There were mutterings in the court, the judge banged his gavel for silence. This man is in denial was the general consensus.

The counsel for the prosecution wasn't sure how to proceed, they had the evidence, the revenue men were queuing up to state on oath that they had gathered this evidence from the plaintiff's address, the evidence was here on the table, and yet this fool was still denying it, did that mean he was going to play 'while the balance of the mind was disturbed' card and plead insanity?

The counsel for the prosecution needed time to think.

"Your witness, I think, "he smiled at the counsel for defence as if to say, the best of luck.

The counsel for the defence rose, he looked far more relaxed than his colleague.

"Mister Wood, let me make it quite clear, for the benefit of the jury, you are charged not with the illegal production of pork scratchings, the production of pork scratchings per se is not a crime, but you are charged with the deliberate evasion of taxes imposed by our lords and masters in London on said products, you have pleaded not guilty. Do you still wish to proceed on that basis?"

"Of course."

"Good." The counsel for the defence sensed victory.

At random and with some theatre the counsel selected a packet from the table.

"Permission to approach the bench my Lord, if I may?"

Permission was granted.

"The learned judge accepted the packet.

"Please study the exhibit my Lord, and tell me what you see."

The judge didn't understand.

"Do you have in your hand a packet of pork scratchings?"

The judge bridled, "Of course I do, that is not in question!"

The counsel smiled indulgently. "Oh, but both my client and myself think that is the question, my Lord, a very important question upon which hangs the outcome of this trial."

Not giving the judge time to bluster, counsel for the defence – who was really rather enjoying himself – continued. He picked up another two packets, quite by random, one of which he tossed across to the prosecution. He smiled and studied the label that Wilf had only recently decided to have printed on the packets, as we have said he had reasoned that now that the

business was ticking over very nicely, almost professionally you might say it should have a professional presentation.
"If my Lord – and my learned colleague would indulge me I will read the label... for the benefit of the jury."
He read the label out loud....

Wilf's PiggyBits.
A Tasty Snack For All TheFamily.
A local cottage industry

"Am I right, My Lord, is that what it says?"
The judge nodded, he didn't see where this was going but he was intrigued enough to let it run.
Prosecution was frowning, what is going on?
Counsel for Wilf continued.
"My Lord, is there anywhere on that label where it states that the contents are pork scratchings?"
So that's where it is going, the judge began to take an interest.
"Of course not, my Lord, why would there be, because they are not pork scratchings, they may bear a passing resemblance to pork scratchings as indeed you might say that a tram bears a passing resemblance to a trolley bus but I put it to you, My Lord, that Mister Wood cannot possibly be defrauding the revenue of any duties whatsoever as he does not make pork scratchings, he makes Wilf's PiggyBits – and I have checked upon this of course at the highest level – there are no duties of any description payable on 'Wilf's PiggyBits, which he has never denied he produces, and why should he, 'a tasty snack for all the family'. I should add in defence of my client that he does not market Wilf's PiggyBits as pork scratchings as this would contravene the trades description act, trying to pass one product off as another and as my client is a law abiding citizen and would never do that, I am sure."
He paused for effect, his job was done.
"The defence rests, My Lord."

The judge was gob-smacked, he motioned for the two counsellors to approach the bench where a whispered conversation took place over several minutes, once or twice looking as if it was quite heated. Finally the judge waved them back to their places.

He coughed to clear his throat.

"Mister Wood, although it is my personal opinion that this court has been made to look a complete fool, in which I include myself, I have to conclude that there is no evidence that you have been making pork scratchings which attract a heavy duty instead you have been making Wilf's PiggyBits – which you have never denied, and as counsel for the defence has pointed out, why should you - which attract none at all. My conclusion is therefore aside from my court being used for a bit of fun, you have committed no offence whatsoever and therefore I have no option but to clear you of these charges against you. Mister Wilfred Wood you will leave this court a free man without a stain on your character, but I ask you in future to play the game.

Wilf raised his hand.

"Yes, Mister Wood, you may speak."

"Your Honour, it has never been my intention to have a bit of fun as you put it with either you or your court, I would not be so dis-respectful; it is not I who couldn't be bothered to read the labels on the little bags, that discrepancy was down to the revenue men who in their impatience to gain a result and perhaps even promotion at my expense failed to take notice of the evidence, or should I say lack of evidence. Had they read the label I feel sure they would have agreed with your learned appraisal of the situation…"

The judge faced the counsel for the prosecution.

"As would certain court officials. I take back what I said about you perhaps making fun of my court, Mister Wood, you have my blessing to go forth and prosper in your venture."

Wilf bowed to the court and left the dock a free man. He was cheered from the courtroom held shoulder high, he was a hero.

In conclusion

The celebrations went on into the night, 'Wilfs PiggyBits' were the toast of the town, publicans, shopkeepers and school canteen mangers queued up to place their order, there was no need for secrecy any longer.

Enoch and Eli painted the company logo on the side of the butcher's bike trailer even managing to spell if correctly. Everywhere that trailer went it raised a cheer from passers-by. Wilf found a small but ideal ex-bagwash laundry complete with working boilers on the industrial estate not far from where they lived – lived for the moment that is, Pru had other ideas in that direction, an inside lavvy and a garden would be nice. They soon had the laundry exactly right for the full-scale production of 'Wilf's PiggyBits'.

Jumping ahead to the future a little, on Enoch's seventeenth birthday Wilf bought a little Austin Seven van for deliveries, the butcher's bike and trailer was placed pride of place on a plinth just inside the main entrance to the PiggyBits factory to remind everyone of their humble beginnings.

The government looked on greedily as 'Wilf's PiggyBits' went national followed almost immediately by international, although they knew only too well that had they tried to subject this product to the forces of purchase tax and export duty imposed on more traditional pork scratchings not only would they have a riot on their hands but they would be guaranteed to lose the next general election, with almost certainly prior to that the enforced resignation of the prime minister.

No wonder the Great British Public voted to leave the EU, God help anyone who tries to mess with our way of life.

Printed in Great Britain
by Amazon

33687238R00078